PIANO · VOCAL · GUITAR

George Harrison
The Apple Years 1968-75

ISBN 978-1-4950-0248-9

7777 W. BLUEMOUND RD. P.O. BOX 13819 MILWAUKEE, WI 53213

For all works contained herein:
Unauthorized copying, arranging, adapting, recording, Internet posting, public performance,
or other distribution of the printed music in this publication is an infringement of copyright.
Infringers are liable under the law.

Visit Hal Leonard Online at
www.halleonard.com

George 1969 (© Harrison Family)

Wonderwall sessions Bombay (© Harrison Family)

Photograph by Terry O'Neill

Wonderwall sessions Bombay (© Harrison Family)

George in front of a fireplace painted by the Fool at his home Kinfauns in Esher 1967 (© Harrison Family)

8	All Things Must Pass	152	I'd Have You Any Time
12	The Answer's at the End	155	If Not for You
21	Apple Scruffs	160	Isn't It a Pity
26	Art of Dying	168	It Is "He" (Jai Sri Krishna)
34	Awaiting on You All	165	It's Johnny's Birthday
31	Ballad of Sir Frankie Crisp (Let It Roll)	172	Let It Down
40	Bangla Desh	177	The Light That Has Lighted the World
46	Be Here Now	182	Living in the Material World
51	Behind That Locked Door	190	The Lord Loves the One (That Loves the Lord)
54	Beware of Darkness	197	Maya Love
58	Bye Bye Love	202	Miss O'Dell
70	Can't Stop Thinking About You	206	My Sweet Lord
76	Dark Horse	214	Ooh Baby (You Know That I Love You)
65	The Day the World Gets 'Round	219	Run of the Mill
82	Deep Blue	224	Simply Shady
84	Ding Dong, Ding Dong	234	So Sad
88	Don't Let Me Wait Too Long	229	Sue Me, Sue You Blues
93	Far East Man	240	That Is All
100	Give Me Love (Give Me Peace on Earth)	244	This Guitar (Can't Keep from Crying)
106	Grey Cloudy Lies	252	Tired of Midnight Blue
110	Hari's on Tour (Express)	258	Try Some Buy Some
115	Hear Me Lord	264	Wah-Wah
124	His Name Is Legs (Ladies and Gentlemen)	268	What Is Life
134	I Dig Love	276	Who Can See It
140	I Don't Care Anymore	280	World of Stone
146	I Live for You	271	You

ALL THINGS MUST PASS

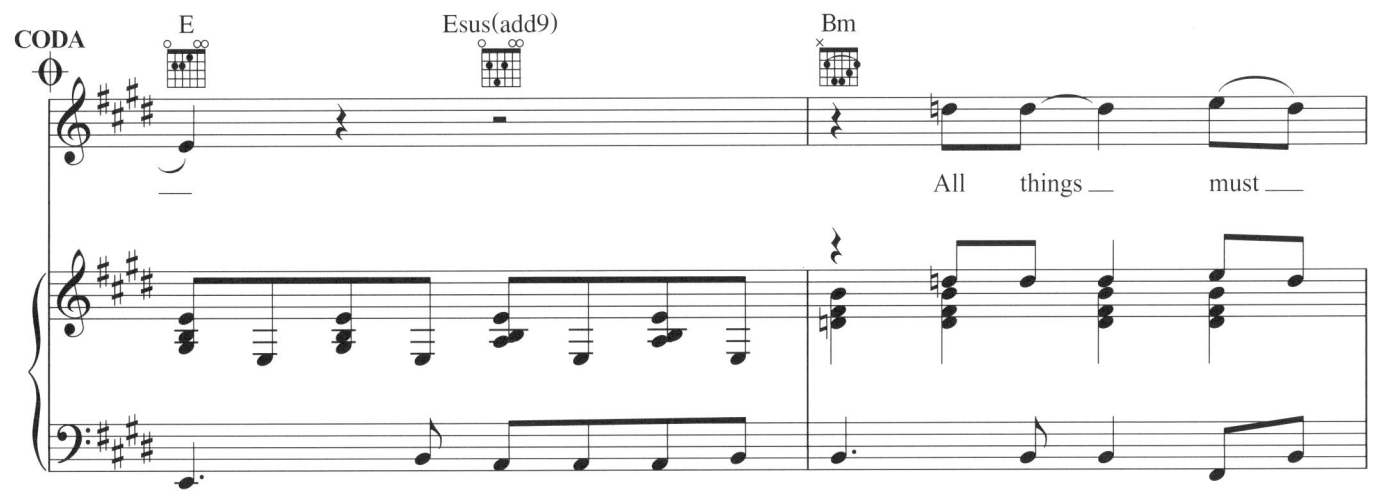
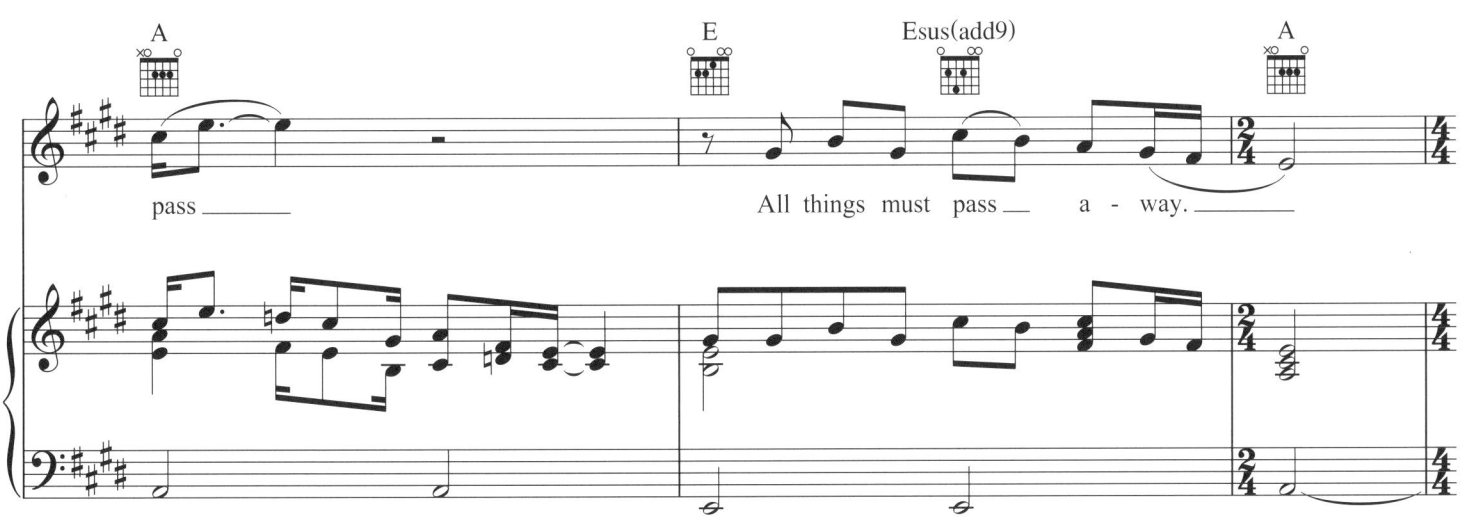
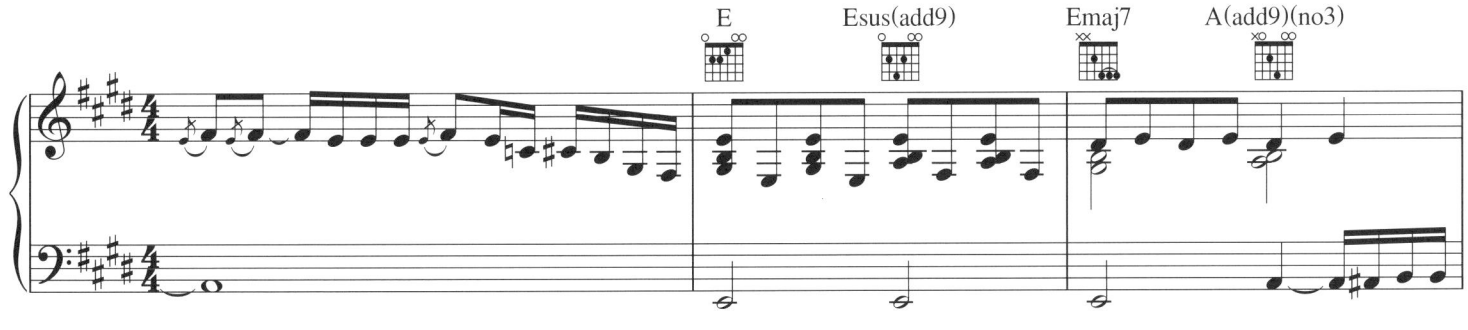
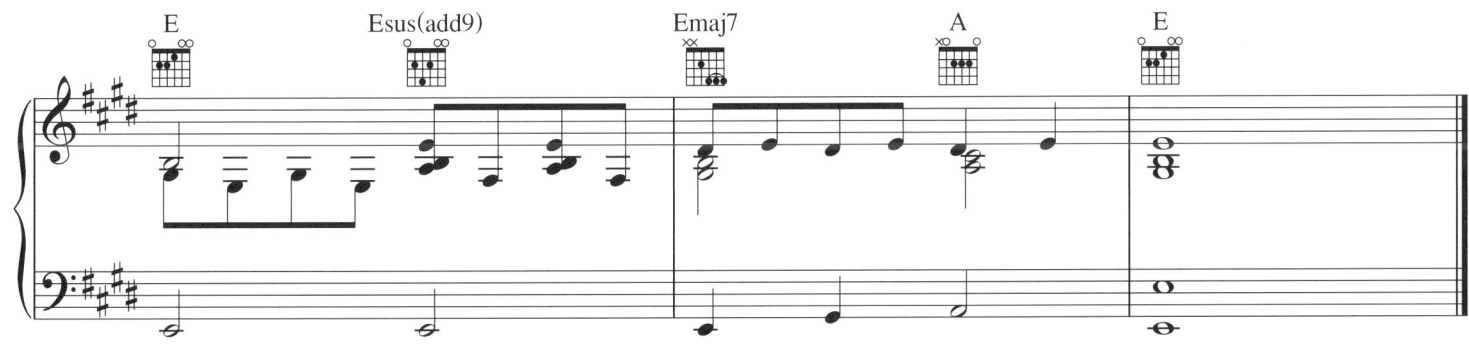

APPLE SCRUFFS

Words and Music by
GEORGE HARRISON

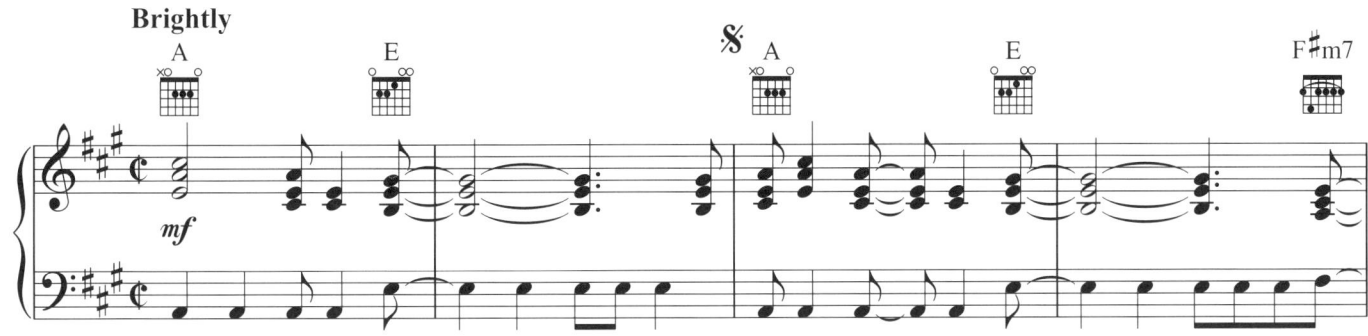
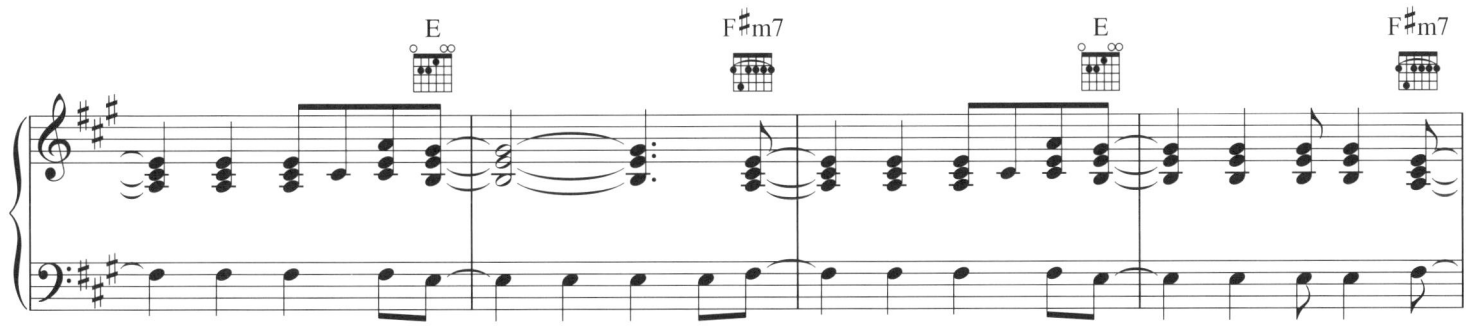
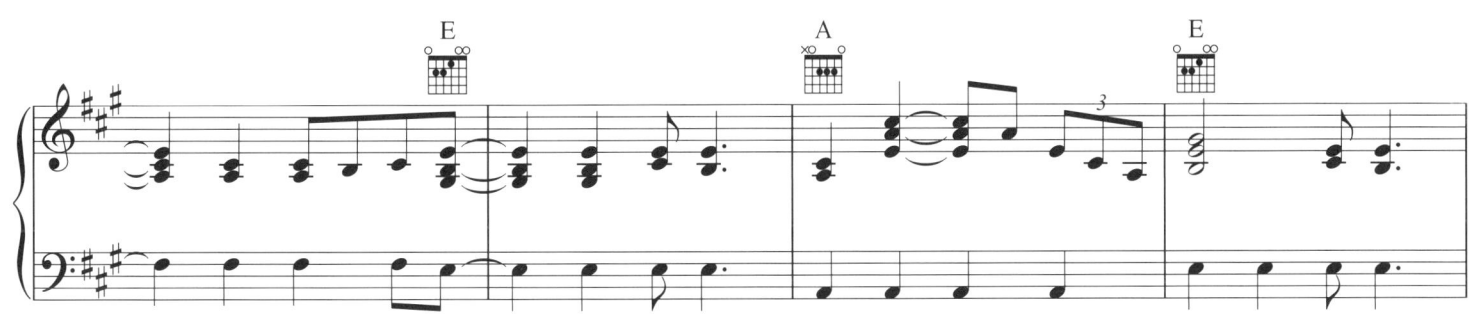

Now I've watched you sitting there,
In the fog and in the rain,
stood around for years,
years, they come and go.

Copyright © 1970 Harrisongs Ltd.
Copyright Renewed 1998
All Rights Reserved

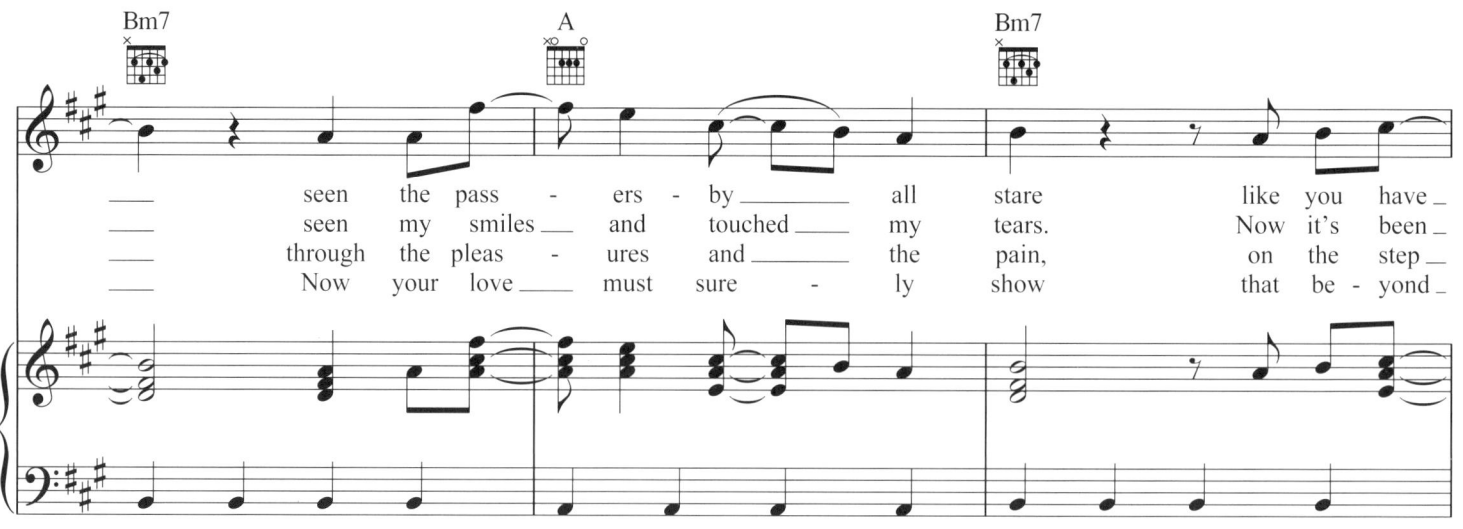

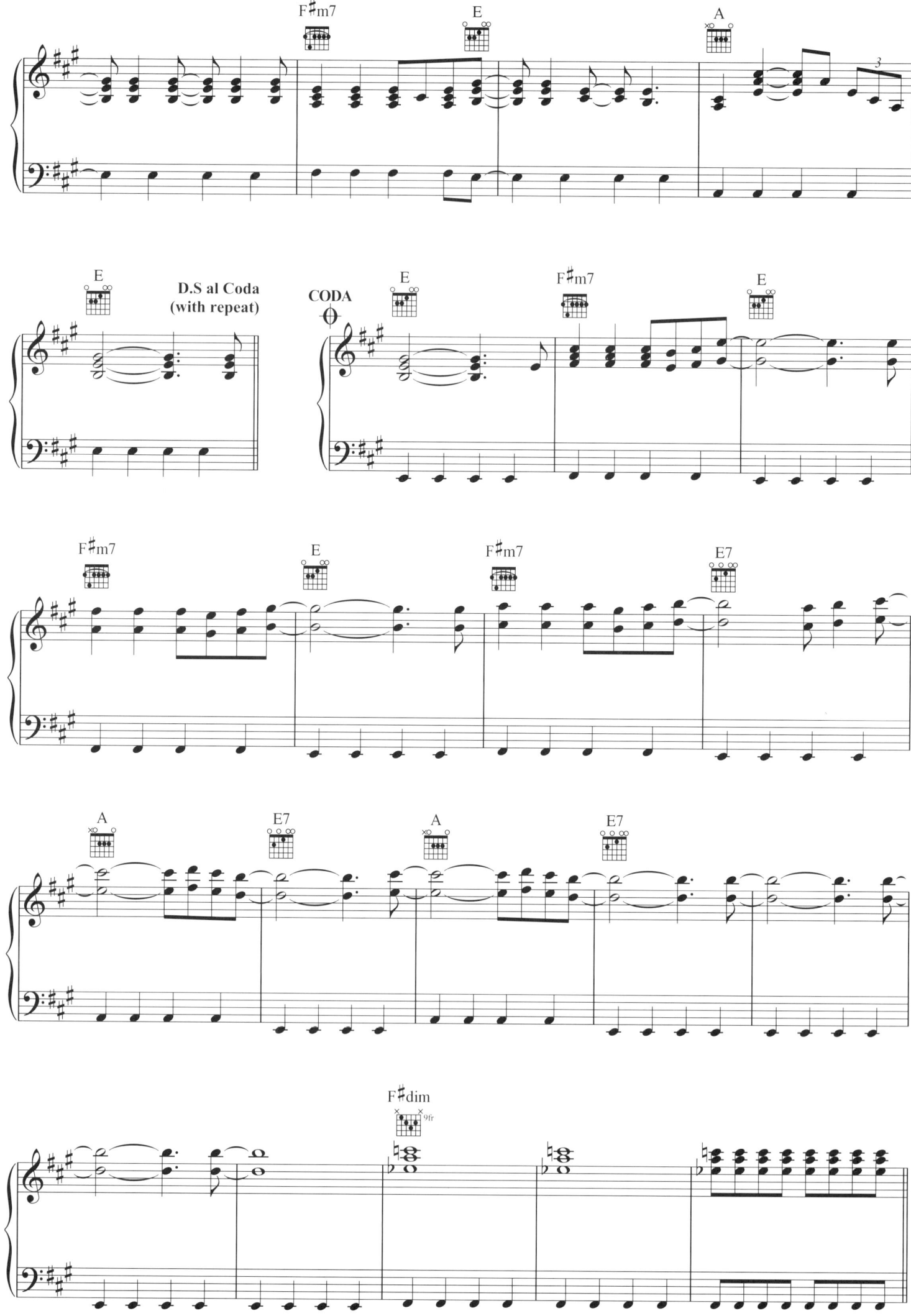

A
Adim
A
Adim
A
Ap - ple scruffs.
Ap - ple scruffs.
F♯m7
B7
how I love you.
How I love you.
A
E
A
E
F♯m7
E
F♯m7
E
F♯m7
E
Repeat and Fade

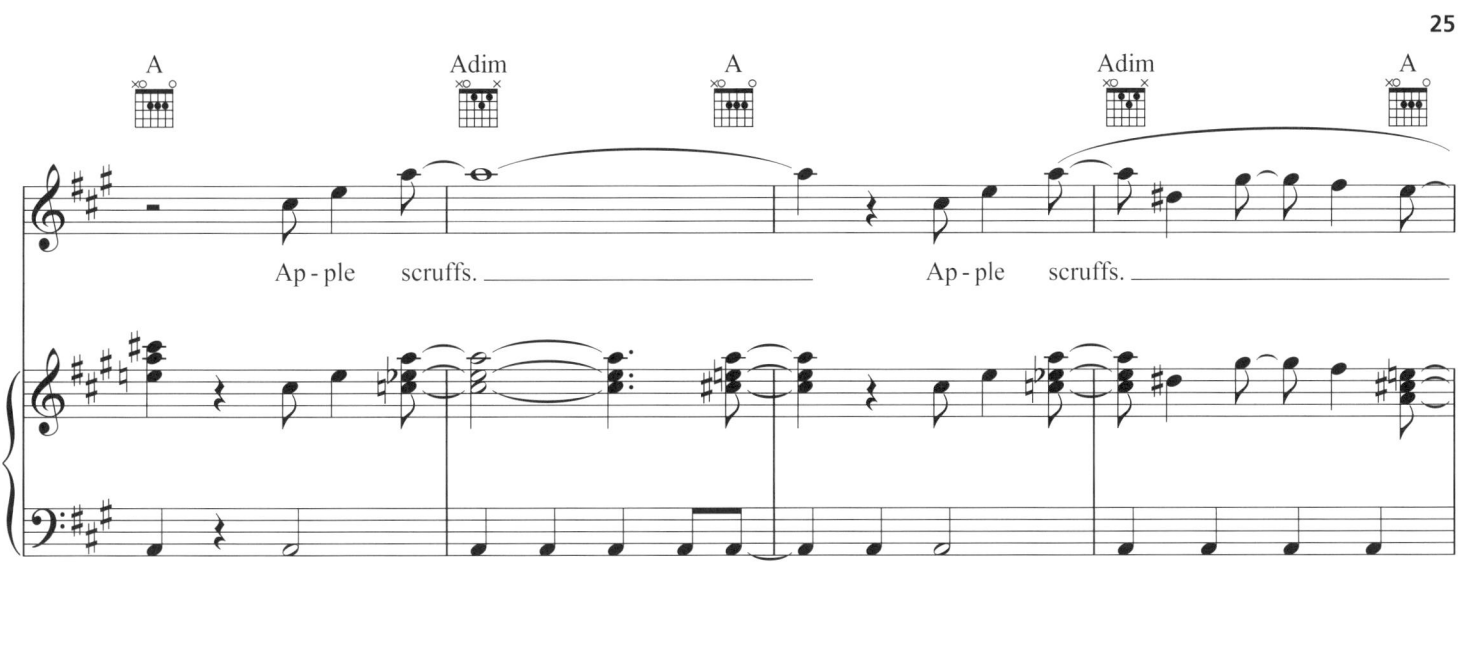

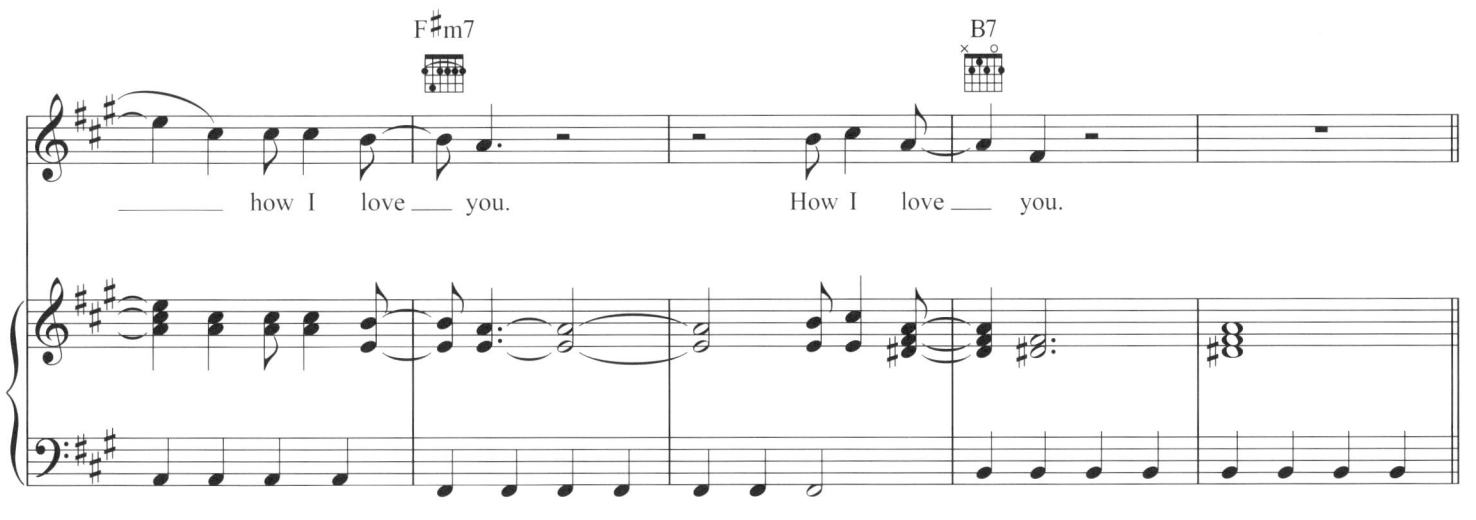

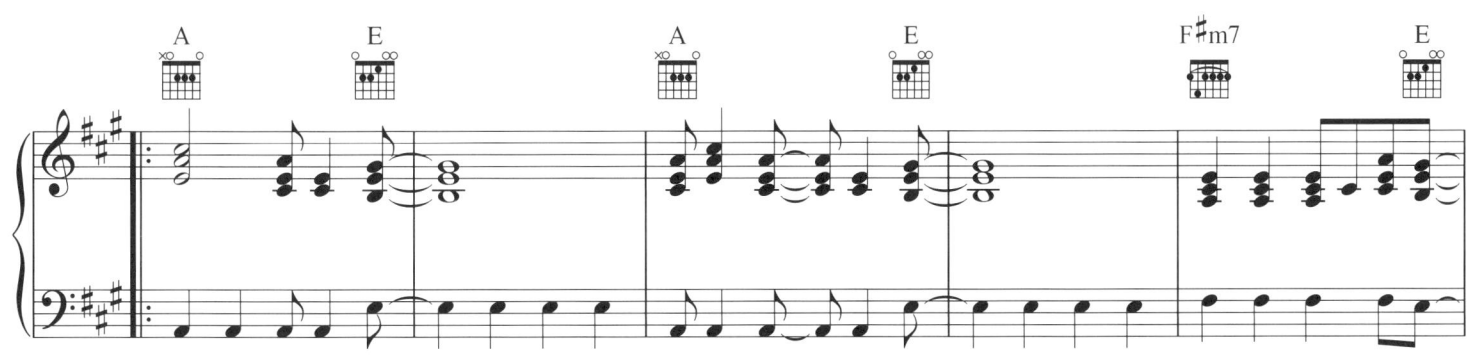

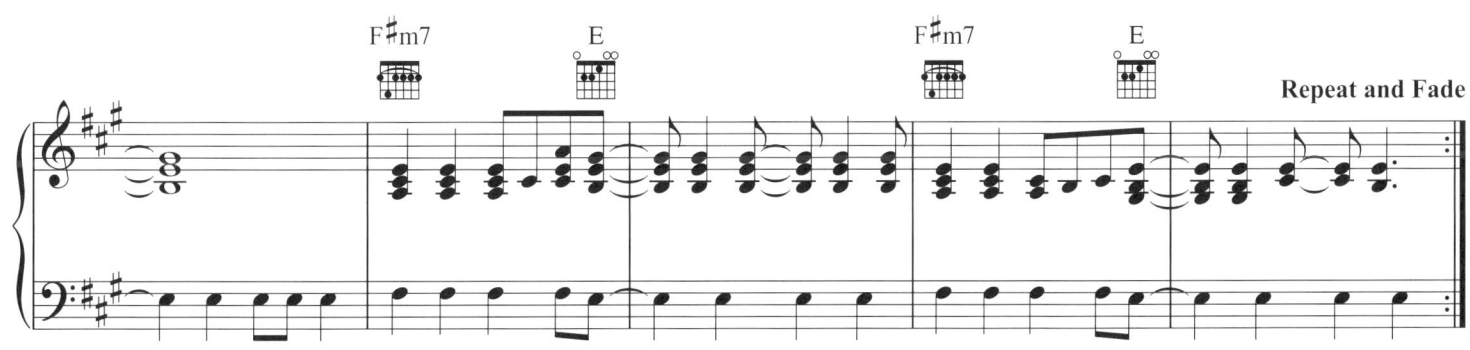

ART OF DYING

Words and Music by
GEORGE HARRISON

Moderate Rock

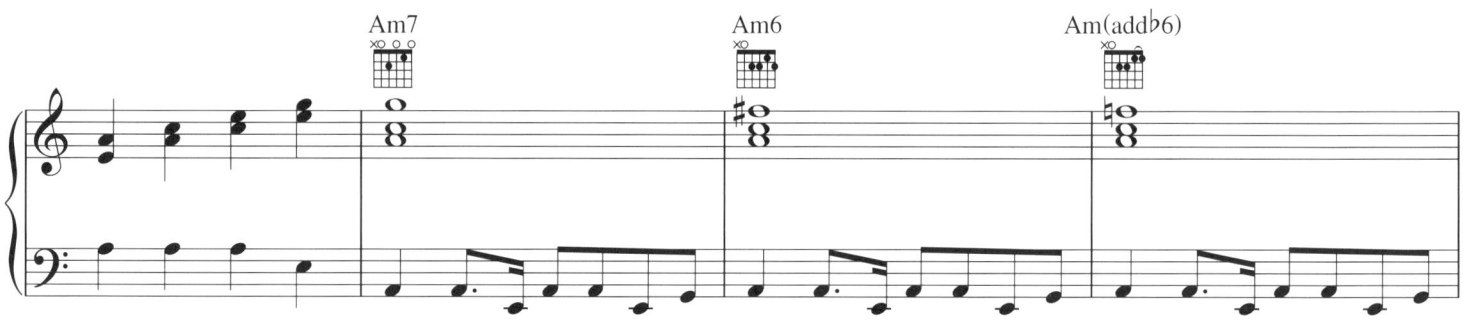

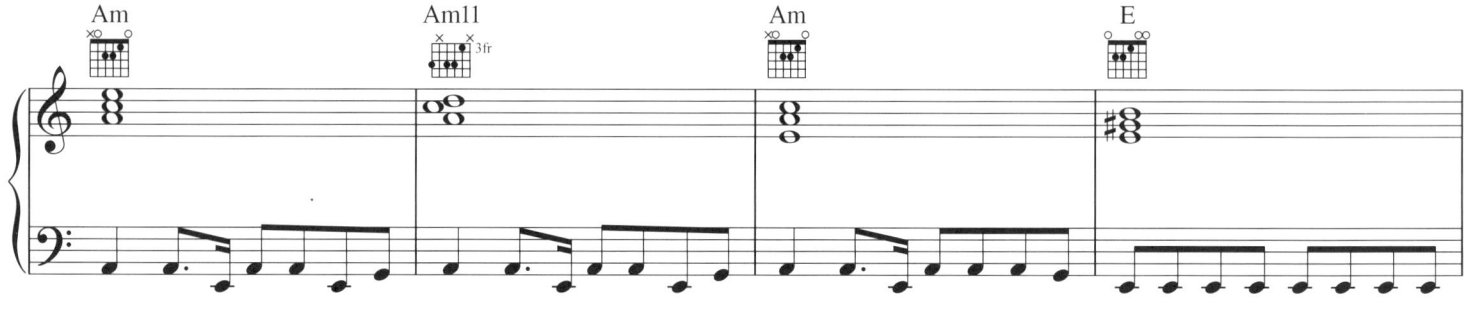

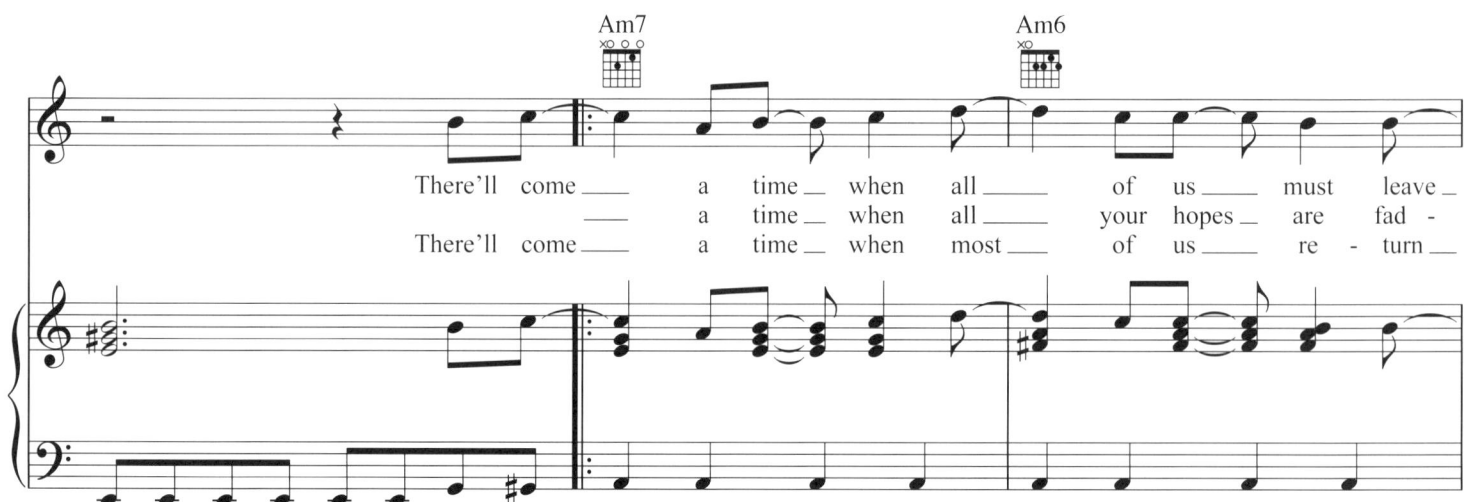

There'll come ___ a time ___ when all ___ of us ___ must leave ___
___ a time ___ when all ___ your hopes ___ are fad-
There'll come ___ a time ___ when most ___ of us ___ re-turn ___

Copyright © 1970 Harrisongs Ltd.
Copyright Renewed
All Rights Reserved

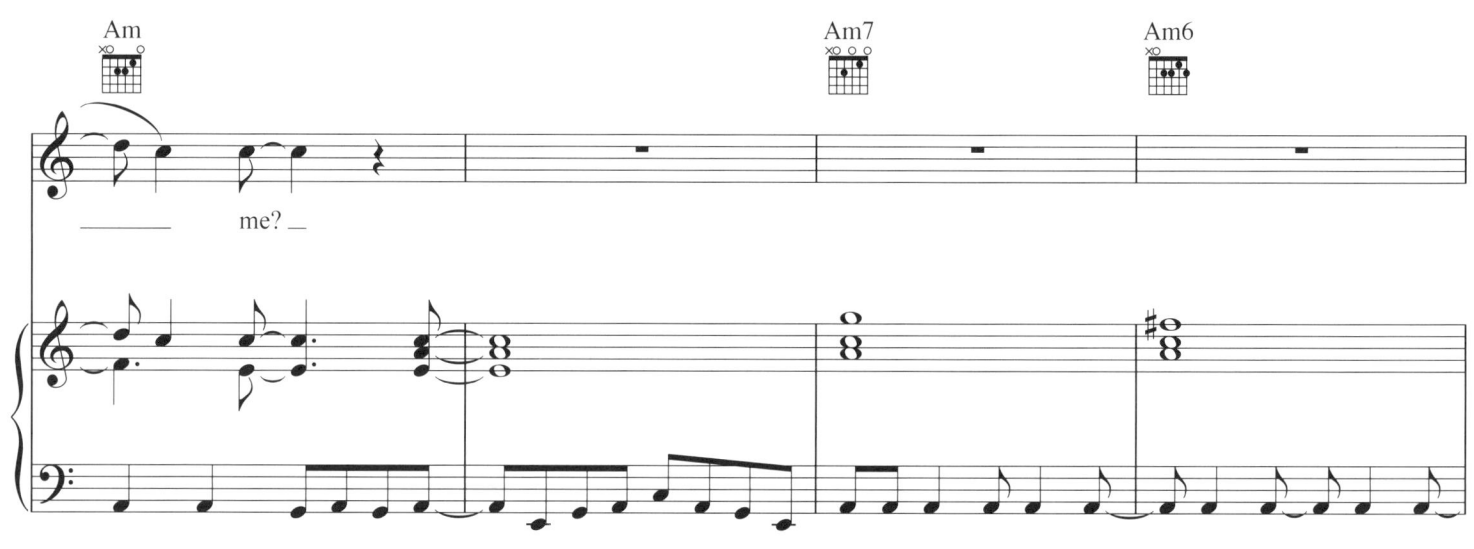
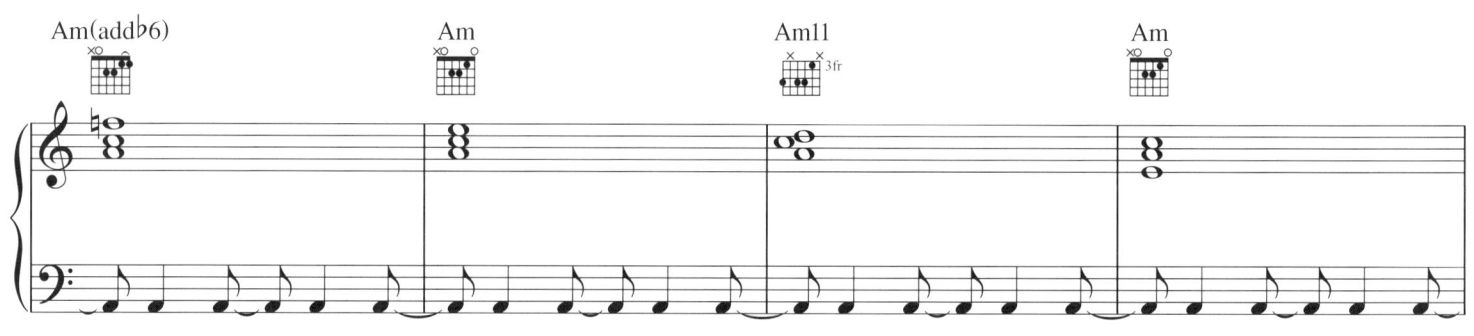

BALLAD OF SIR FRANKIE CRISP
(Let It Roll)

Words and Music by
GEORGE HARRISON

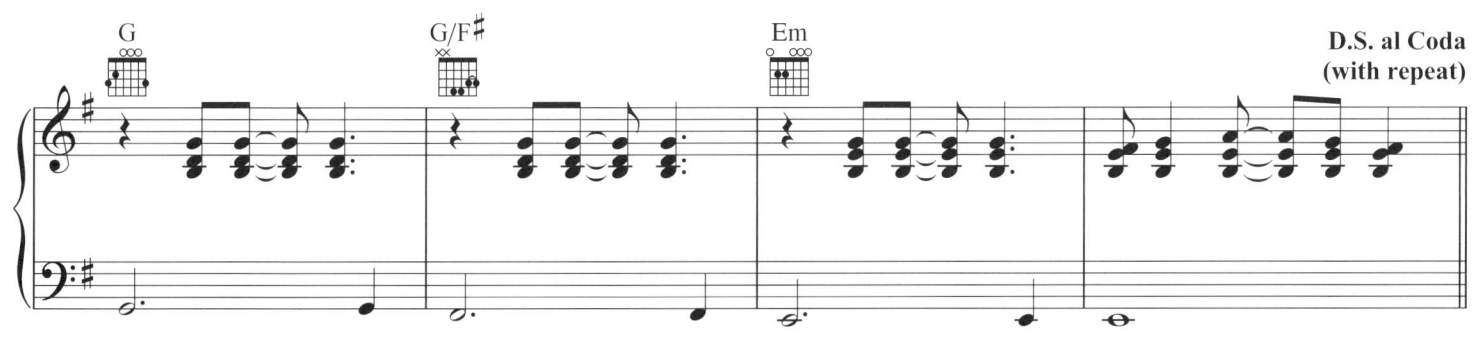
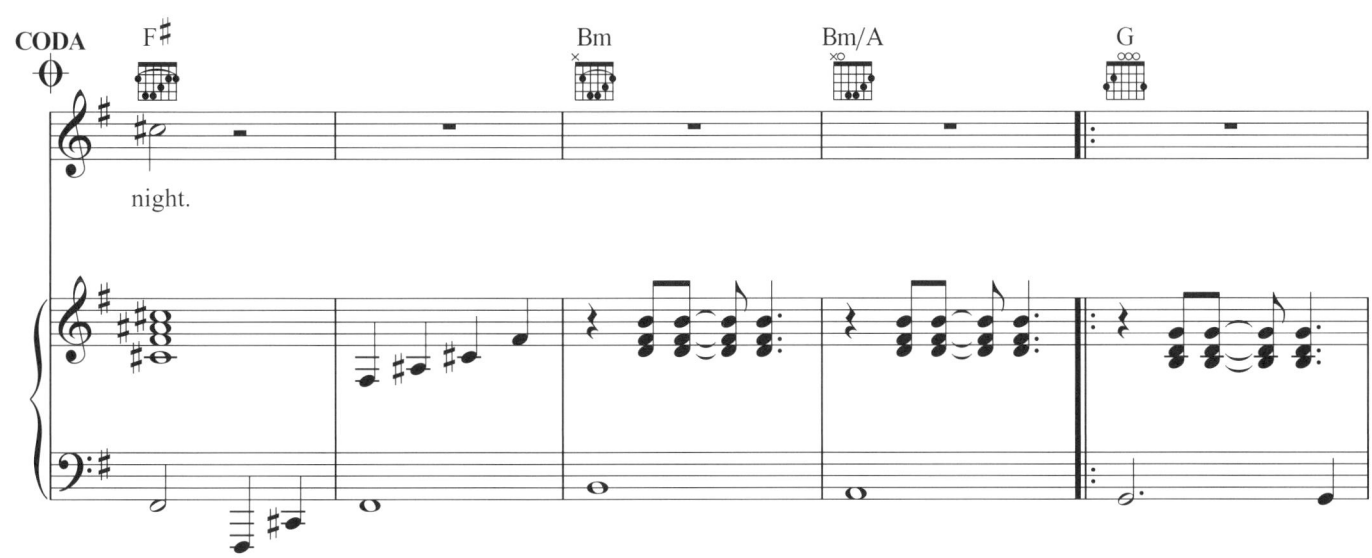
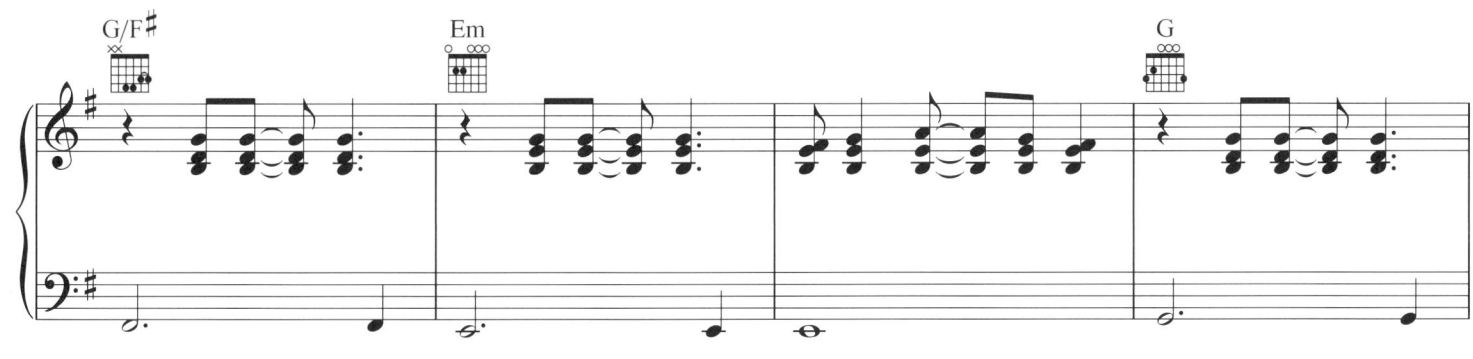
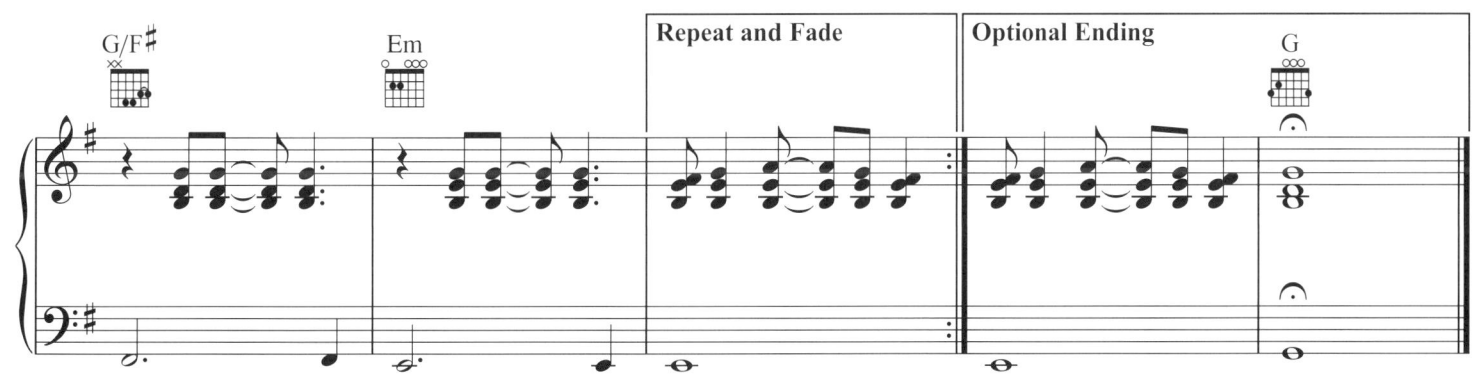

AWAITING ON YOU ALL

Words and Music by
GEORGE HARRISON

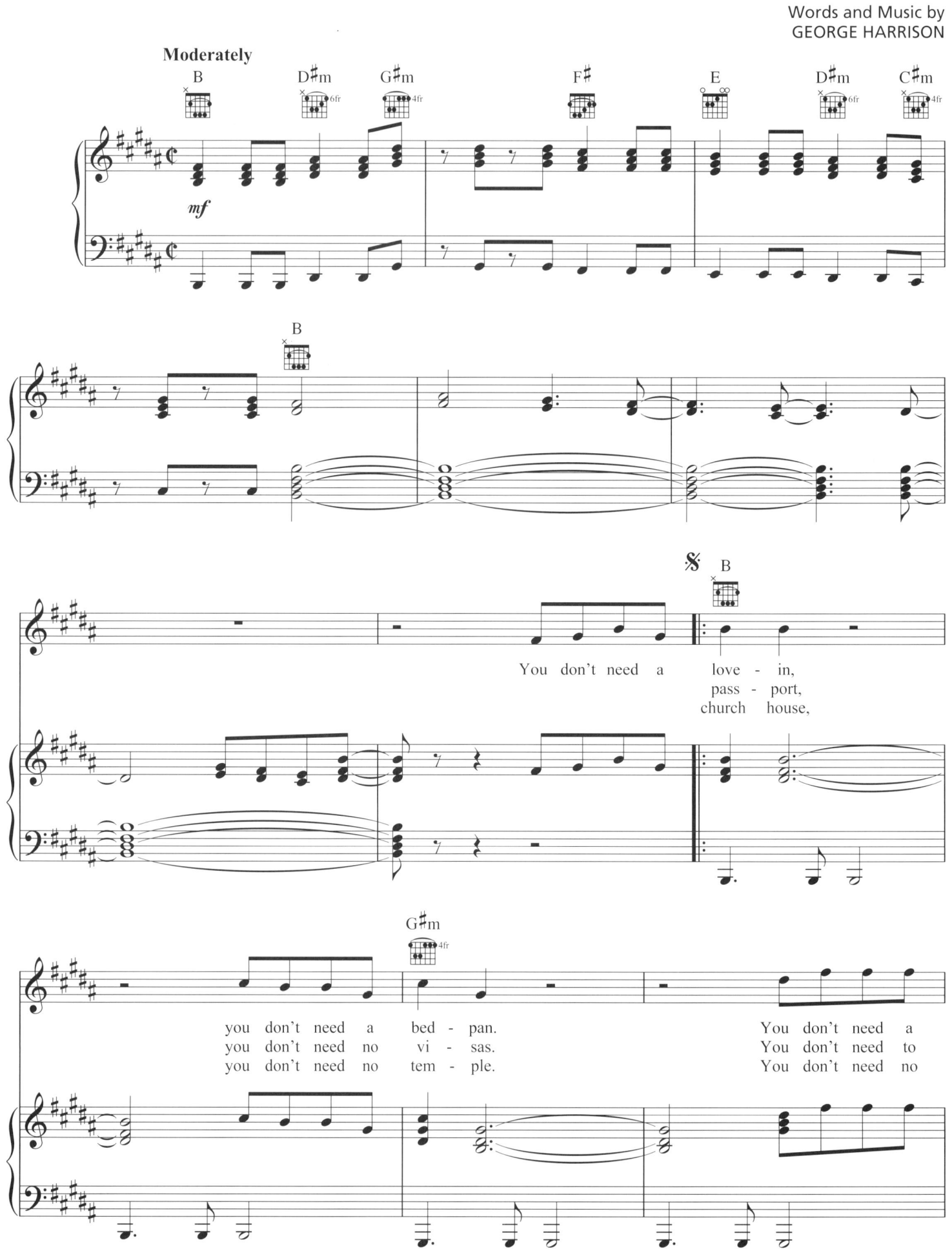

Copyright © 1970 Harrisongs Ltd.
Copyright Renewed
All Rights Reserved

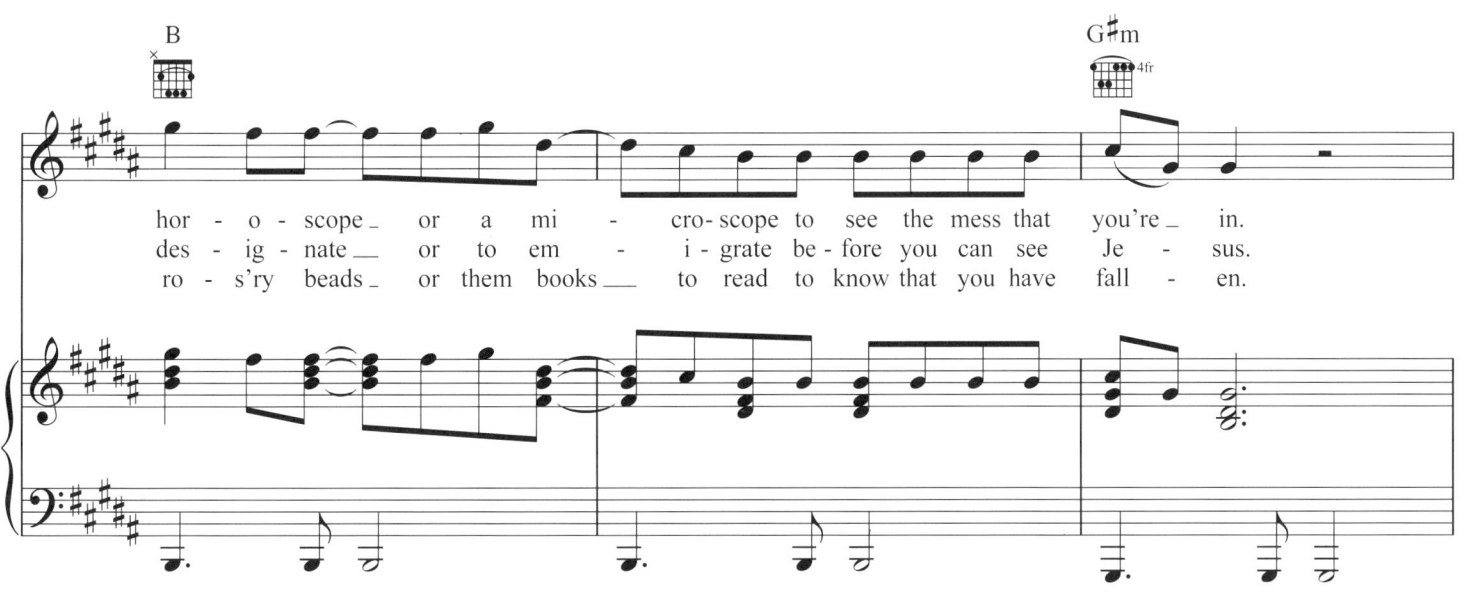

Lord, and you'll be free. The
Lord is a-waiting on you all to a-wak-en and see.

You don't need no   You don't need no

D.S. al Coda

all ___ green, ___ while the Pope owns fif-ty-one ___ per-cent of Gen-er-al Mo-tors, and the stock ex-change __ is the on-ly thing he's qual-i-fied to quote us. But the Lord is a-wait-ing on you

D♯m C♯m B D♯m G♯m F♯
6fr 4fr 6fr 4fr
all to a - wak - en and see.
By
E D♯m C♯m B D♯m G♯m
6fr 4fr 6fr 4fr
chant - ing the names of the Lord, and you'll be free.
F♯ E D♯m C♯m B
6fr 4fr

BANGLA DESH

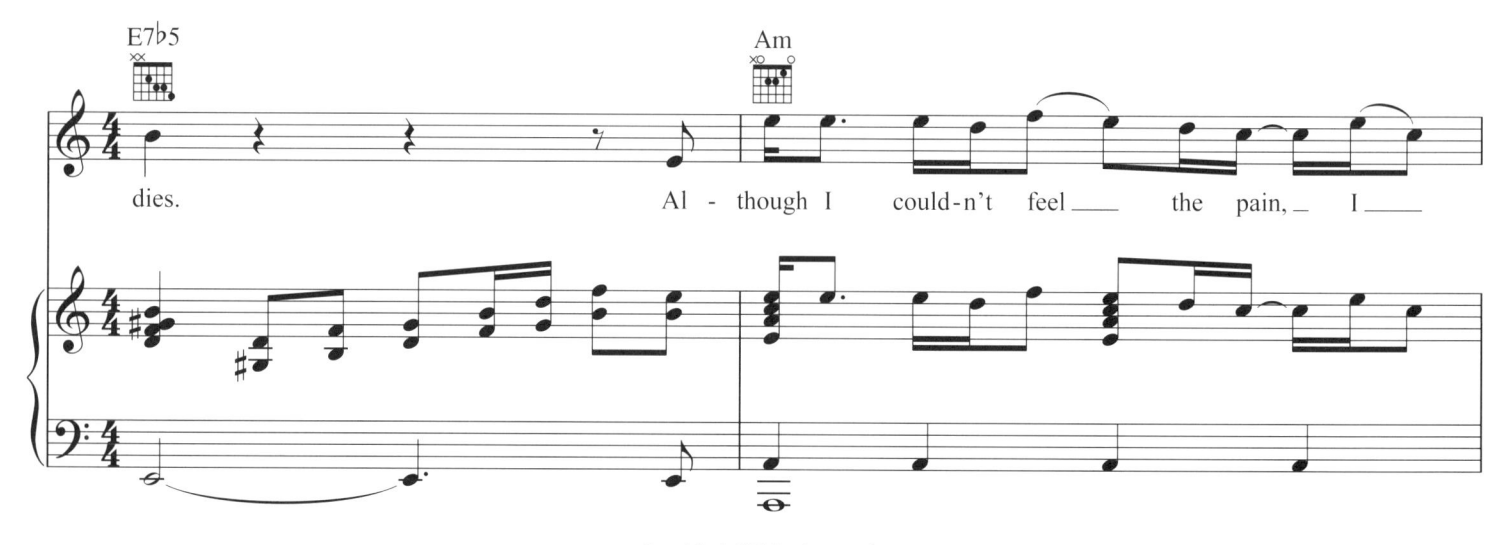

Words and Music by
GEORGE HARRISON

My friend came to me with sadness in his eyes.
Told me that he wanted help before his country dies.
Although I couldn't feel the pain, I

Copyright © 1971 Harrisongs Ltd.
Copyright Renewed
All Rights Reserved

knew I had to try. Now I'm asking all of you to help us save some lives.

Moderately

1. Ban - gla - desh,
2. Ban - gla - desh,
3. *Instrumental*
4. Ban - gla - desh,

Ban - gla - desh, where so
Ban - gla - desh, such a
Ban - gla - desh, now it

man - y ____ peo - ple ____ are dy - ing ____ fast, ____ and it sure
great dis - as - ter ____ I don't un - der - stand, ____ But it sure
may seem ____ so far ____ from where we ____ all are. ____ It's some - thing

Dm

looks like a mess. ____ I've nev - er
looks like a mess. ____ I've nev - er
we can't re - ject. ____ That suf - f'ring

G#7

seen such ____ dis - tress. ____
known such ____ dis - tress. ____ Now, won't ____ you
I can't ____ ne - glect. ____ Now, please ____ don't
Now, won't ____ you

E

lend your ____ hand; ____ try to un - der - stand. ____ Re - lieve the peo -
turn a - way. ____ I wan - na hear you ____ say, ____ "Re - lieve the peo -
give some ____ bread? ____ Get the starv - ing ____ fed. ____ We've got to re -

-ple of Bangladesh.

-ple of Bangladesh."

-lieve. Bangladesh.

Re-lieve the peo-

-ple of Ban - gla - desh.

We've got to

re - lieve Ban - gla - desh.

Now won't you lend your hand and under-stand. Relieve the peo- ple of Ban- gla- desh.

Repeat and Fade

BE HERE NOW

Words and Music by
GEORGE HARRISON

Slowly and gently

With pedal

Re - mem - ber
Now

now.
is

Be here
here

Copyright © 1973 Harrisongs Ltd.
Copyright Renewed
All Rights Reserved

A5
Asus2
A5
Asus2
D(add2)
now, as it's not
now, and it's not
Amaj7/C♯
like it was be - fore.
what is was be - fore.
Bm7
E
The past,
Re -
A5
A6
mem - ber
was.
now.
Be
5fr

Amaj7
A5
here
now,
Asus2
A5
Asus2
D(add2)
Amaj7/C♯
as it's not
what
like
it was
Bm7
E
be - fore
A5
it was.

49

A mind that wants to wan-der 'round a cor-ner is an un-wise mind.

BEHIND THAT LOCKED DOOR

Words and Music by
GEORGE HARRISON

Moderate Country Waltz

Why are you still cry-ing? Your pain is now through.
smil-ing. What else should we do?

Please for-get those tear - drops, let me take them from you.
With on-ly this short time, I'm gon-na be here with you.

The love you are
And the tales you have

Copyright © 1970 Harrisongs Ltd.
Copyright Renewed
All Rights Reserved

blessed with, this world's wait-ing for.
taught me, from the things that you saw,

So, let out your heart please, please, from be-hind that locked
makes me want out your heart

door. It's time we start

And if ev-er my love goes, if I'm rich or I'm poor, please let out my heart please, please, from be-hind that locked door, from be-hind that locked door.

BEWARE OF DARKNESS

Words and Music by
GEORGE HARRISON

Moderately slow, in 2

Watch out, now. Take care. Beware of fall-
Watch out, now. Take care. Beware the thoughts
Watch out, now. Take care. Beware of soft-
Watch out, now. Take care. Beware of greed-

-ing swing-ers
that lin-ger,
shoe shuf-flers
-y lead-ers.

They'll

Copyright © 1970 Harrisongs Ltd.
Copyright Renewed 1998
All Rights Reserved

drop - ping all a - round you. The pain
wind - ing up in - side your head. The hope -
danc - ing down the side - walks. As each
take you where you should not go. While weep -

that of - ten min - gles in your fin -
- less - ness a - round you in the dead
un - con - scious suf - f'rer wan - ders aim -
- ing at las ce - dars, they just want

- ger - tips. Be - ware of

dark - ness.

of night.
-less-ly,

Be-ware of sad-ness. It can hit you.
be-ware of Ma-ya. *Instrumental*

It can hurt you, make you sore.

And what is more, that is not what you are

57

BYE BYE LOVE

Words and Music by FELICE BRYANT
and BOUDLEAUX BRYANT

Copyright © 1957 by HOUSE OF BRYANT PUBLICATIONS, Gatlinburg, TN
Copyright Renewed
All Foreign Rights Controlled by SONY/ATV MUSIC PUBLISHING LLC
All Rights for SONY/ATV MUSIC PUBLISHING LLC Administered by SONY/ATV MUSIC PUBLISHING LLC, 424 Church Street, Suite 1200, Nashville, TN 37219
International Copyright Secured   All Rights Reserved

D
Am7
Am
E7
Am7
Hel - lo lone - li - ness,
I think I'm gon - na cry.
D
Am7
Bye bye love.
D
Am7
D
Bye bye sweet car - ess.
Hel - lo
Am7
Am
E7
Am7
emp - ti - ness.
I know I'm gon - na die.
Good - bye

60

| Am | E7 | Am7 | Am | N.C. |

my love, __ bye bye. __ There goes __ our la-

| E7 |

-dy __ with a "you know who." __

| Am7 | D | E7 |

I hope __ she's hap - py, __

| Am7 |

old "Clap - per" too. ____

D

We had good rhythm. Then she stepped in,

E7

did me a favour. I

Am7   **C**
                            N.C.

threw them both out.

D   **Am7**   **D**   **Am7**

Good-bye hap-pi-ness,

D
Am7
Am
E7
Am7
hel - lo lone - li - ness. I think I'm gon - na cry. Bye
Am
E7
Am7
N.C.
Am7
bye my love, bye bye.
(Lead vocal ad lib.)
D
Play 7 times
Am
E7
Am7
Am
E7
Am7
Good - bye my love, good - bye.
N.C.
E7
Now I'm in - to ro - mance,

I shy a-way from love.

Got tired of lad-ies that plot and shove

me. That's the rea-son we all can see.

They see that our la-dy is

out on a spree.　　Bye bye love.
　　　　　　　　　　Bye bye love.

Bye bye hap - pi - ness.　　Hel - lo lone - li - ness.
Bye bye hap - pi - ness.　　Hel - lo emp - ti - ness.

Think I'm gon', think I'm gon', I'm gon - na cry.

Repeat and Fade

(Lead vocal ad lib.)

Optional Ending

THE DAY THE WORLD GETS 'ROUND

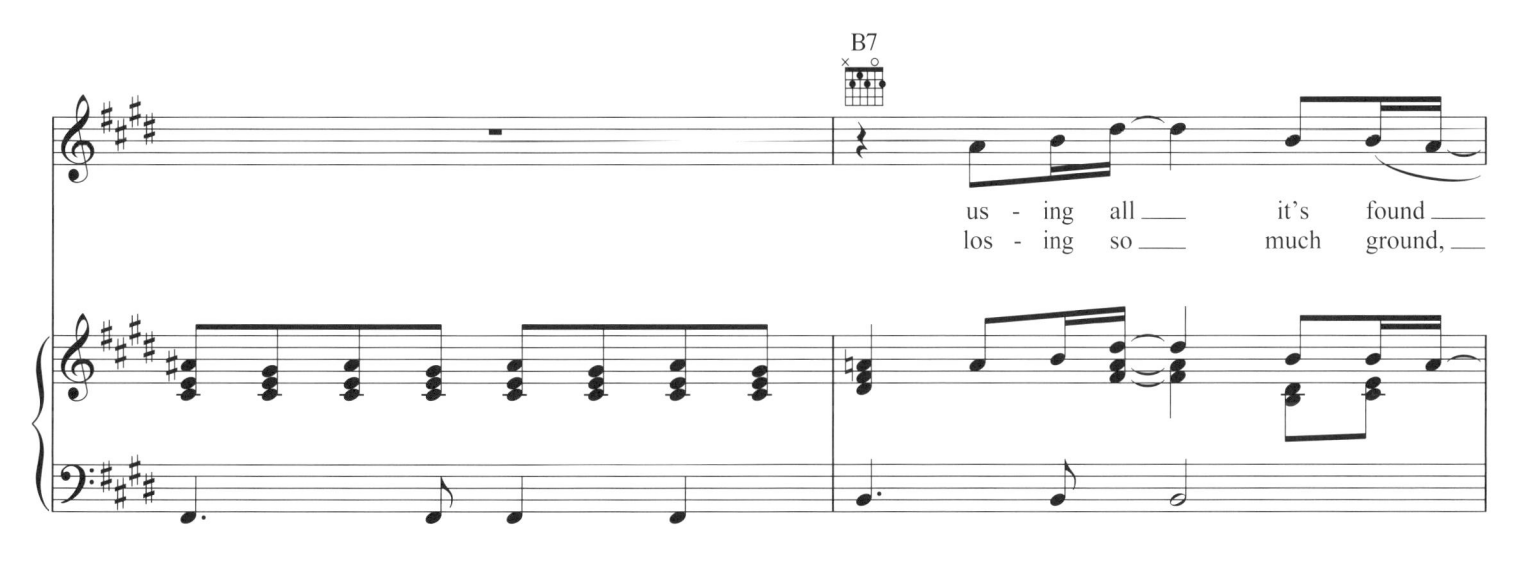

Words and Music by
GEORGE HARRISON

to help each other, hand in
killing each other, hand in

hand. The

hand. Such

fool - ish - ness in man! I want no part

of ___ their plan, ___ no! ___

If you're the de-struc-tive kind, ___ now I'm work-ing from day ___ to day, ___

as I don't wan-na be ___ like you. ___

I look for the pure ___ of heart, ___ and the ones who have made ___ a start. ___

B
E/B
But Lord, there are just a few
B
A
D/A
A
D/A
who bow be-fore you.
In si-lence they pray.
A
E
B
E
Oh, how they pray for the day the world gets
F♯7sus
F♯7
'round...

using all __ they've found __ to help __ each oth - er, hand ____ in hand. ____ The day the world gets 'round. ____

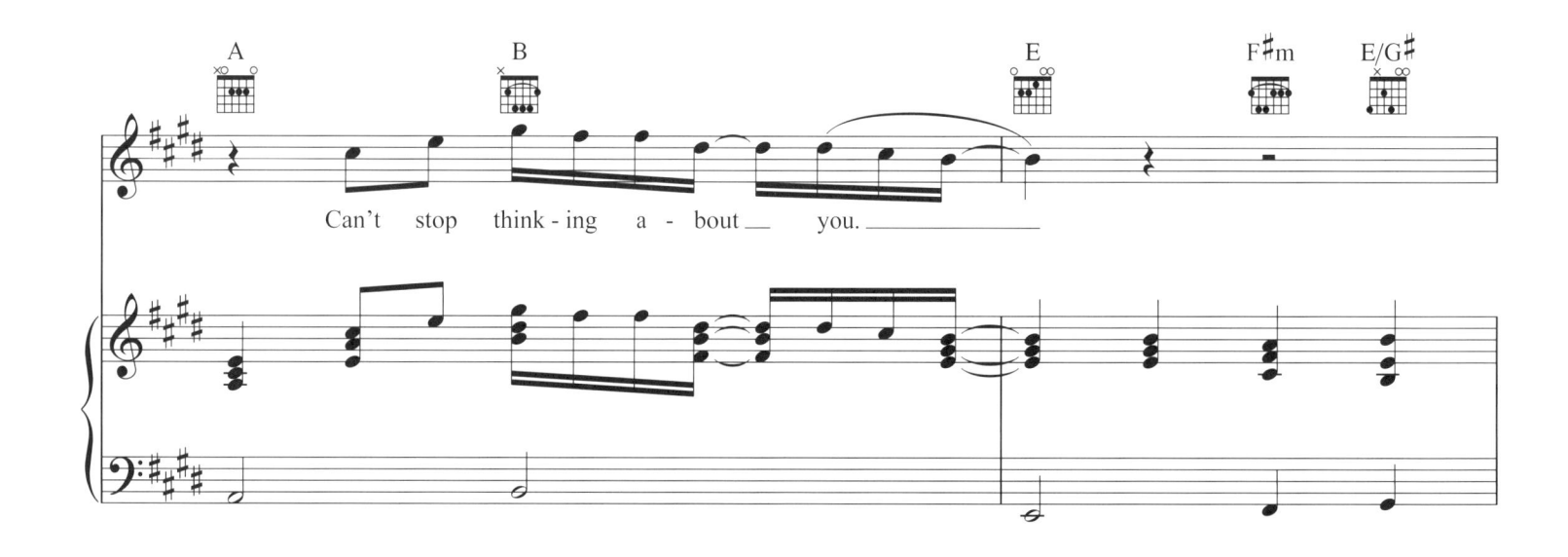

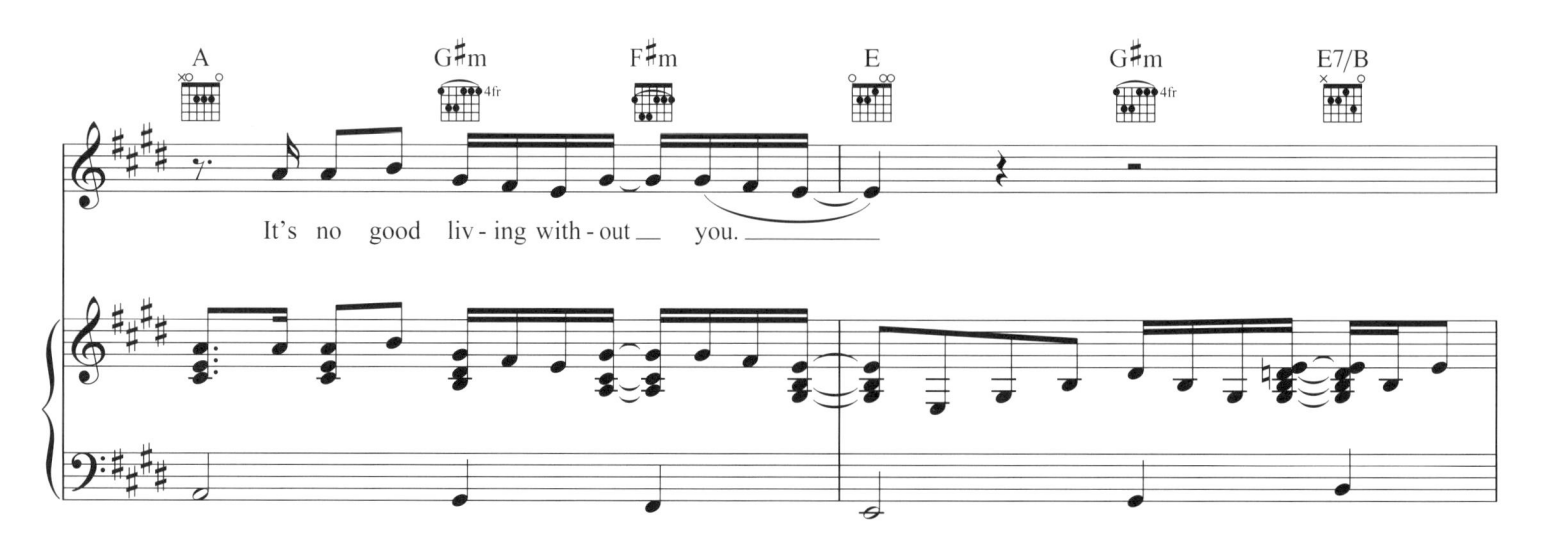

ނ# CAN'T STOP THINKING ABOUT YOU

Words and Music by
GEORGE HARRISON

Moderate Ballad

Can't stop thinking about you.

Can't stop thinking about you.

It's no good living without you.

Copyright © 1975 Umlaut Corporation
Copyright Renewed
All Rights Reserved

I can't stop thinking about you.

Can't stop thinking about you.

Can't stop thinking about you.

And it's no good living without you.

A
B
E
I can't stop think-ing a-bout you.
When the night-
Emaj7
E7
E/D♯
E/D
- time comes a - round.
- ing comes a - round.
C♯+
C♯7
C♯/G♯
4fr
Day - light has left me, I, I can't
And the day - light gets to me, I, I can't
A
F♯7/A♯
4fr
E
C♯m7/F♯
9fr
take it if I don't see you no more.
take it if I don't see you no more.

F♯sus F♯ E/G♯ A F♯7/A♯
I can't help it, need your lov -
I can't help it, need your lov -
E F♯7sus
- ing so much more.
- ing so much more.
8va
C♯m7/F♯ F♯5 G♯5 A G♯m F♯m
And I can't stop think-ing a - bout you.
E G♯m E7/B A B
I can't stop think-ing a - bout you.

E
F♯m
E/G♯
A
G♯m
4fr
F♯m
And it's no good liv-ing with-out you.
E
G♯m
4fr
E7/B
A
B
I can't stop think-ing a-bout,
A
B
A
B
I can't stop think-ing a-bout,
I can't stop think-ing a-bout you.
E
G♯m
4fr
E7/B
A
B
Oh.
I can't stop think-ing a-bout,

75

DARK HORSE

Words and Music by
GEORGE HARRISON

Moderately

You thought that you knew where I was and when
thought that you'd got me in your grip.
thought that you knew it all a - long,

Ba - by, it looks like you're
Ba - by, looks like
un - til you start - ed

fool - in' you a - gain.
you was not so smart.
get - tin' me not right.

You
And

Copyright © 1974 Umlaut Corporation
Copyright Renewed
All Rights Reserved

thought that you __ had got - ten me all __ staked out. __
I be - came __ too slip - p'ry for __ you. __
Seems as if __ you heard __ a lit - tle late. __

Ba - by, it looks __ like I've __ been break - in' out. __
But let me tell, __ you, that __ was noth - in' new.
I warned you when __ we both __ was at the start-

-in' gate.} I'm a dark __

horse

runnin' on a dark race-course.

I'm a blue moon

since I stepped out of the womb.
since I picked up my first spoon.
since I stepped out of the womb.

79

You horse.

horse.

D.S. al Coda

CODA

horse.

DEEP BLUE

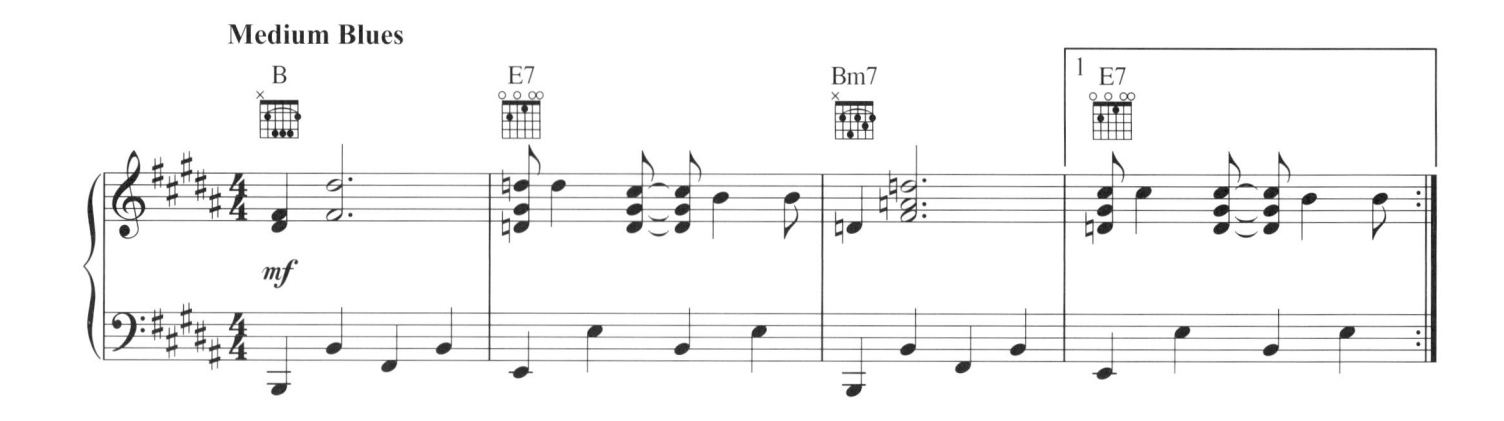

Words and Music by
GEORGE HARRISON

Medium Blues

When the sun-shine is not e-nough to make me feel bright, it's
stand there watch ti-red bod-ies full of sick-ness and
think of the life I'm liv-in', pray, God help me. Give

got me suf-f'ring in the dark-ness that's so eas-y come by on the
pain to show you just how help-less you real-ly are. When you get
me Your light so I can love You and un-der-stand this rep-e-

Copyright © 1971 Harrisongs Ltd.
Copyright Renewed
All Rights Reserved

Bm7
E7
B
road - side of one long life - time.
down to the truth, it hurts me.
ti - tion that keeps me here feel - in' deep blue.
E7
G
It's got me deep blue. You know, I'm deep blue.
It's got me deep blue. You know, I'm deep blue.
You know, I'm deep blue. You know, I'm deep blue.
E7
To Coda
1, 2
3
D.S. al Coda
When you
When I
When the
CODA
B
E7
Bm7
E7
Repeat and Fade

DING DONG; DING DONG

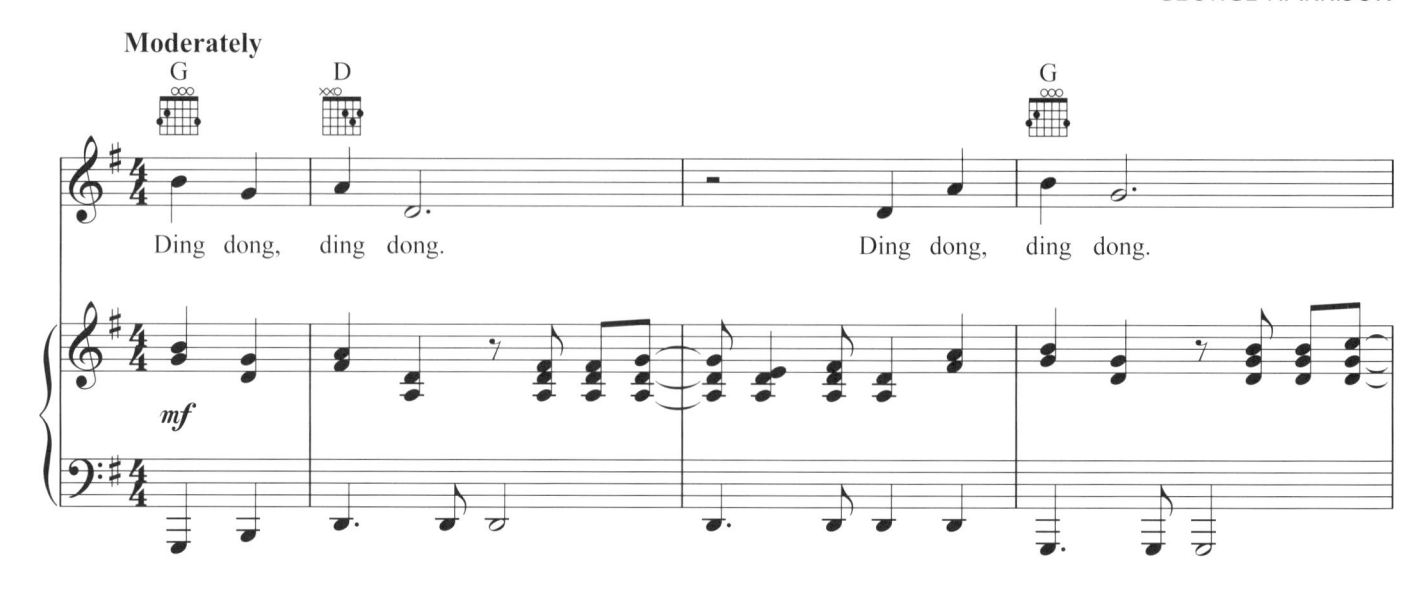

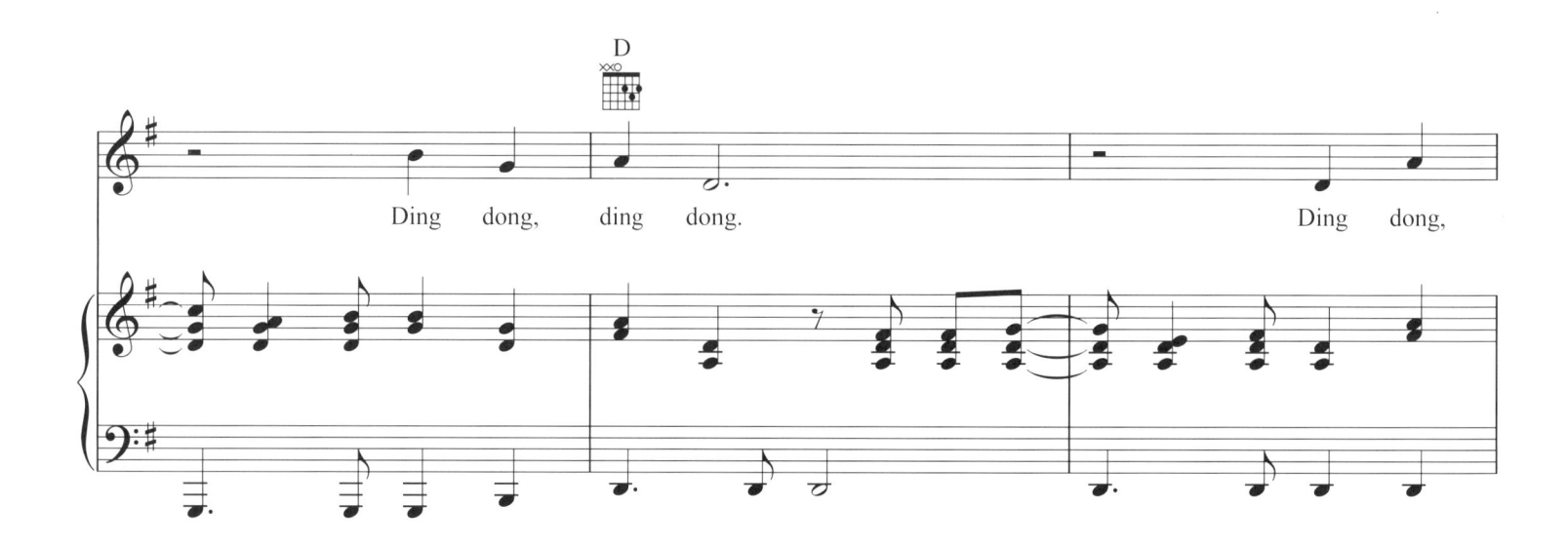

Words and Music by
GEORGE HARRISON

*Copyright © 1974 Umlaut Corporation
Copyright Renewed
All Rights Reserved*

_____ the new. Ring out the old; ring in _____

_____ the new. Ring out the false; ring in _____

_____ the true. _____ Ring out the old; ring in _____

1, 3, 4

_____ the new. _____

86

Ding dong, ding dong. Ding dong, ding dong. Ding dong, ding dong. Ding dong. Ding dong, ding dong.

Yes-ter-day, to-day was to-mor-

87

DON'T LET ME WAIT TOO LONG

Words and Music by
GEORGE HARRISON

Moderately

I _____ love you, _____ ba-by, so don't _____ let me wait _____ too long.

_____ I _____ love you, _____ ba-by, so don't

Copyright © 1973 The Material World Charitable Foundation Ltd. and Harrisongs Ltd.
Copyright Renewed
All Rights Reserved

Gm7
C7
F
let me wait too long.
I miss you,
C7sus
C7
baby, so don't let me wait too long.
F
Gm7
I miss you, baby, so don't let me wait too long
C7
F
till you're here by my side.
Now, only you

know how to dry up all of those tears that I've cried.

Here with your love; now, only you

know how to lay it down like it came { from up above. / from above. }

You know it's you I love.

F
C7sus
Ooh,
1.2. now,
3. so
don't let me wait too long.
C7
F
Ooh,
now,
1
Gm7
C7/G
don't let me wait too long.
2
Gm7
don't let me wait too
C7
long till you're here
D.S.
3
Gm7
C7
don't let me wait too long.

I ___ miss you, ___ baby, so don't ___ let me wait ___ too long. ___

I ___ miss you, ___ baby, so don't ___

___ let me wait, ___ don't ___ let me wait, ___ don't ___ let me wait ___ too

long. ___

FAR EAST MAN

Words and Music by GEORGE HARRISON
and RON WOOD

F♯m7
Emaj7
I won't let him down.
We can't let them down.
F♯m7
Emaj7
Gon - na do what I can.
We got - ta do what we can.
F♯m7
Emaj7
I can't let him drown;
We can't let them drown;
F♯m7
B7sus
2fr
E
he's a far east man.
he's a far east man.

Amaj7
G♯m7
C♯m7
G♯m7
All these ups and those downs
Looks like right here on earth,
Amaj7
G♯m7
C♯m7
Bm7
makes me ques - tion what love real - ly is:
God, it's hell - ish some - times.
Amaj7
G♯m7
C♯m7
G♯m7
Gm7
is it a lie, or worth - while?
I feel that Heav - en's in sight.
F♯m7
Emaj7
I can't let him down.

| F#m7 | Emaj7 |

Got-ta do what I can.

| F#m7 | Emaj7 |

I can't let him drown;

| F#m7 | B7sus | E | **To Coda** |

he's a far east man.

| C#m7 | Gdim7 |

Some-time is so short but it takes so long. I'm

won-d'ring if ___ it is, ___ or if I'm ___ wrong. ___

E- ven then, __ my heart ___ seems __ to be the one __ in charge: __

can on - ly do ___ what ____ it tells ____ me.

(1.) I can't let him down.
(2.) *Instrumental fills*
(3.) I can't let him down.

Gon- na do what I can.
Gon- na do what I can.
I got- ta do what I can.

F♯m7
Emaj7
I can't let him drown;
1, 2
F♯m7
B7sus
2fr
E
he's a far east man.
3
F♯m7
B7sus
2fr
E
F♯m7
He's a far east...
Emaj7
F♯m11
E

GIVE ME LOVE
(Give Me Peace on Earth)

Words and Music by
GEORGE HARRISON

free ___ from birth. Give ___ me hope, help me cope with ___ this heav-y load. ___ Try-ing to ___ touch ___ and reach ___ You with heart and soul. ___ Oh, _____ my ___ Lord. ___

Please take hold of my hand that I might understand You. Won't You please. Oh, won't You Lord.

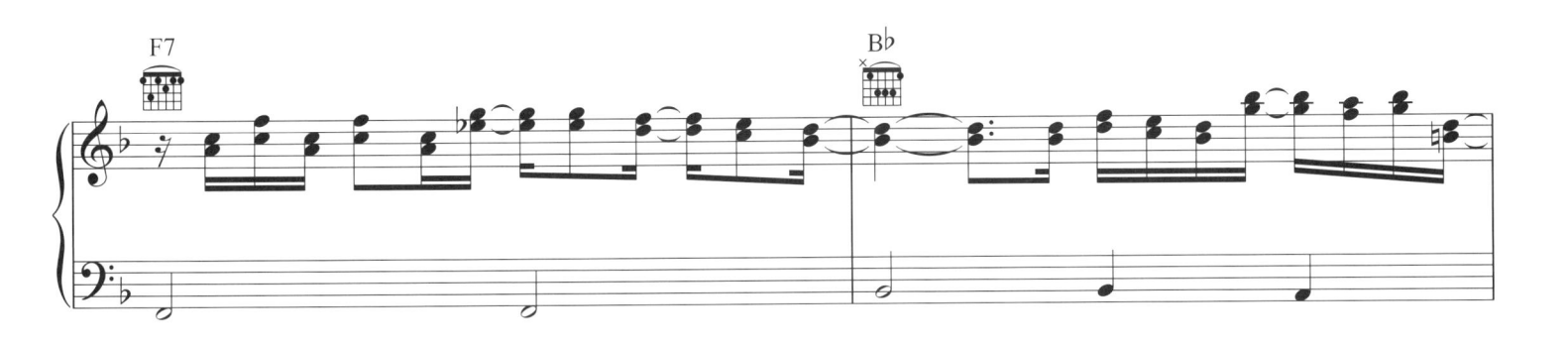

Won't You please. Oh, won't You

Give me love, give me love, give me peace on earth. Give me light, give me life, keep me keep me free from birth. Now give me hope, help me cope with this heavy load. Trying to touch and reach You with heart and soul.

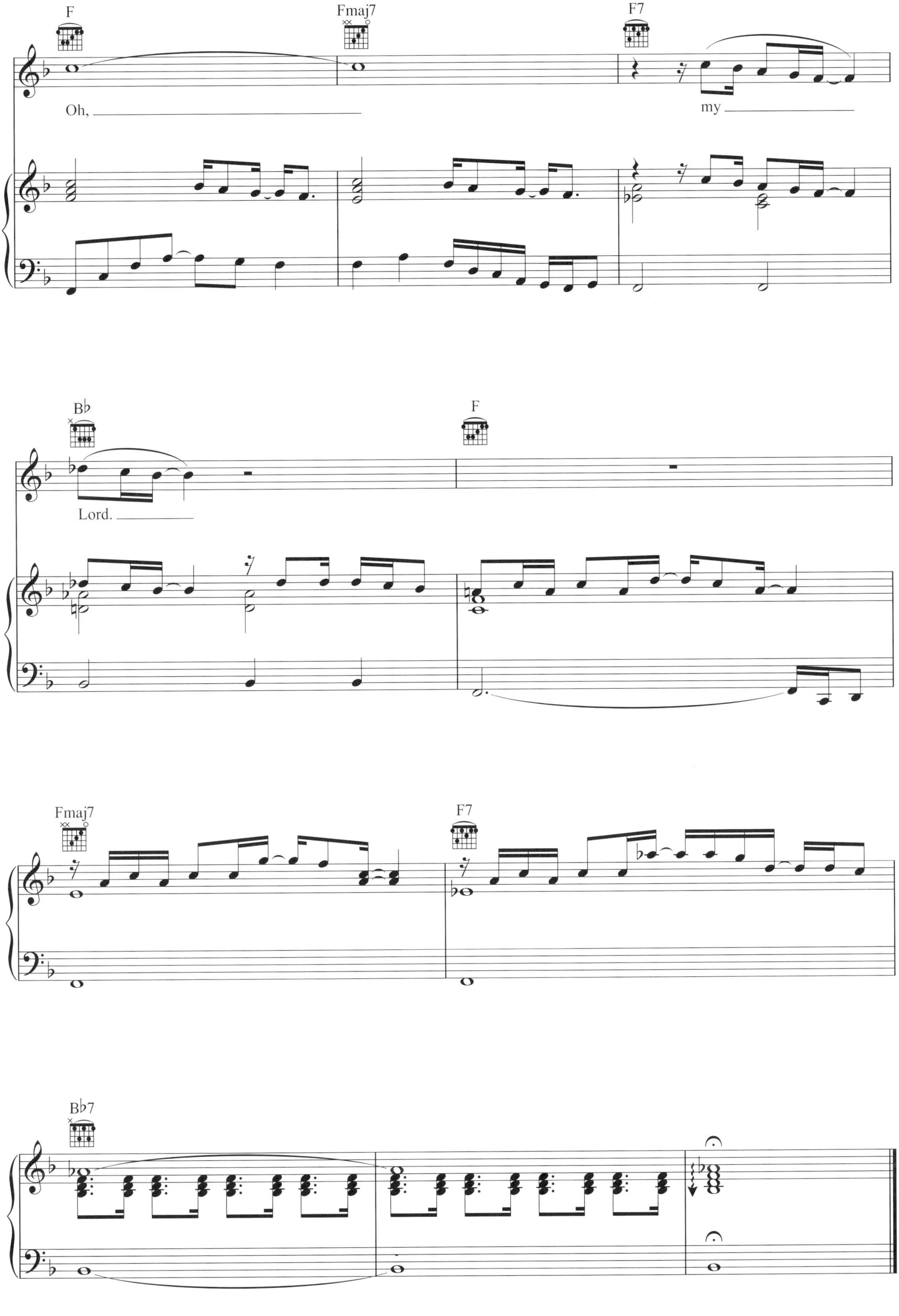
F
Fmaj7
F7
Oh,
my
B♭
F
Lord.
Fmaj7
F7
B♭7

GREY CLOUDY LIES

Words and Music by
GEORGE HARRISON

Ponderously

And I thought to close my mouth with a pad-lock on the night.

Copyright © 1975 Umlaut Corporation
Copyright Renewed
All Rights Reserved

Leave the bat-tle-field be-hind.

Stay out the fight.

Not lose my sight.

Now I only want to be
Now I only want to live
Vocal tacet 3rd time

with no pistol at my brain.
with no tear drops in my eyes.

But at times it gets so lone-
But at times it feels like no

-ly.
chance.

Could go insane.
No clear blue skies.
No clear blue skies.

Could lose my aim.
Grey cloud - y lies.
Grey cloud - y lies.

Repeat and Fade

HARI'S ON TOUR
(Express)

Words and Music by
GEORGE HARRISON

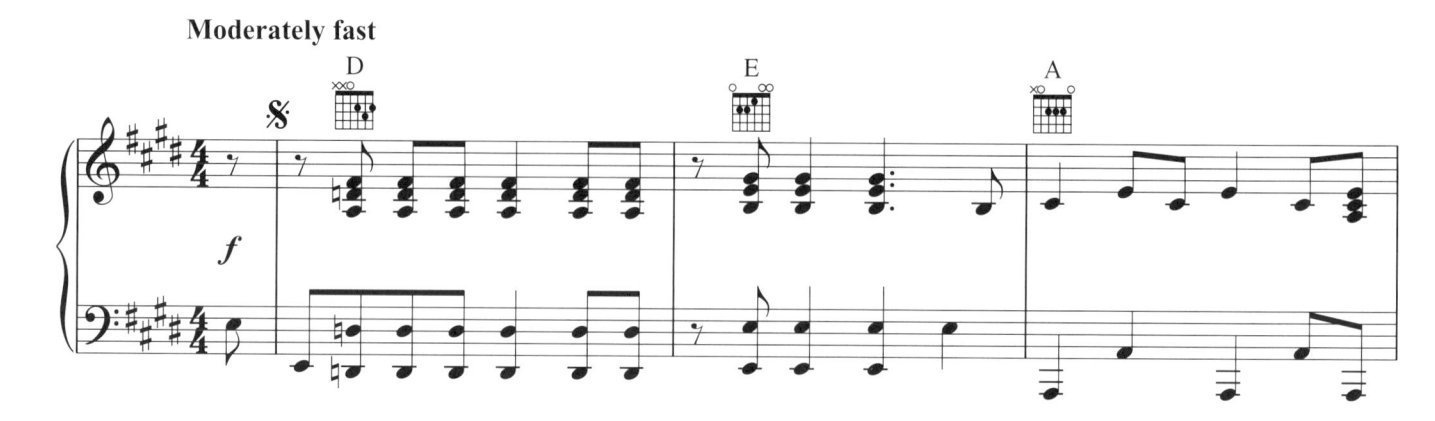

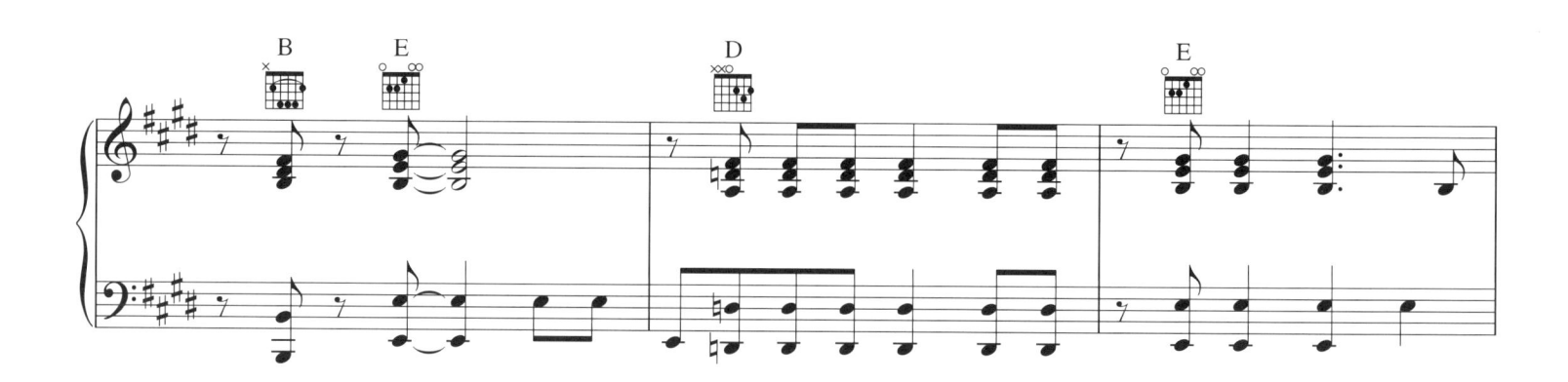

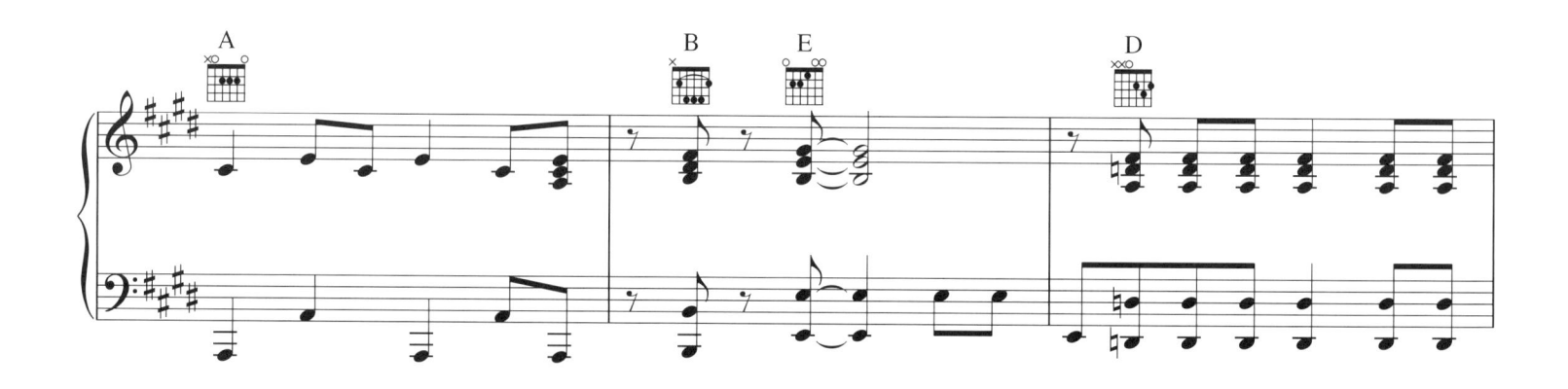

Moderately fast

Half as fast
A
E
A
E
C♯m7
4fr
G♯m7
4fr
A
E
C♯m7
4fr
G♯m7
4fr
A
Tempo I
E
B7
E

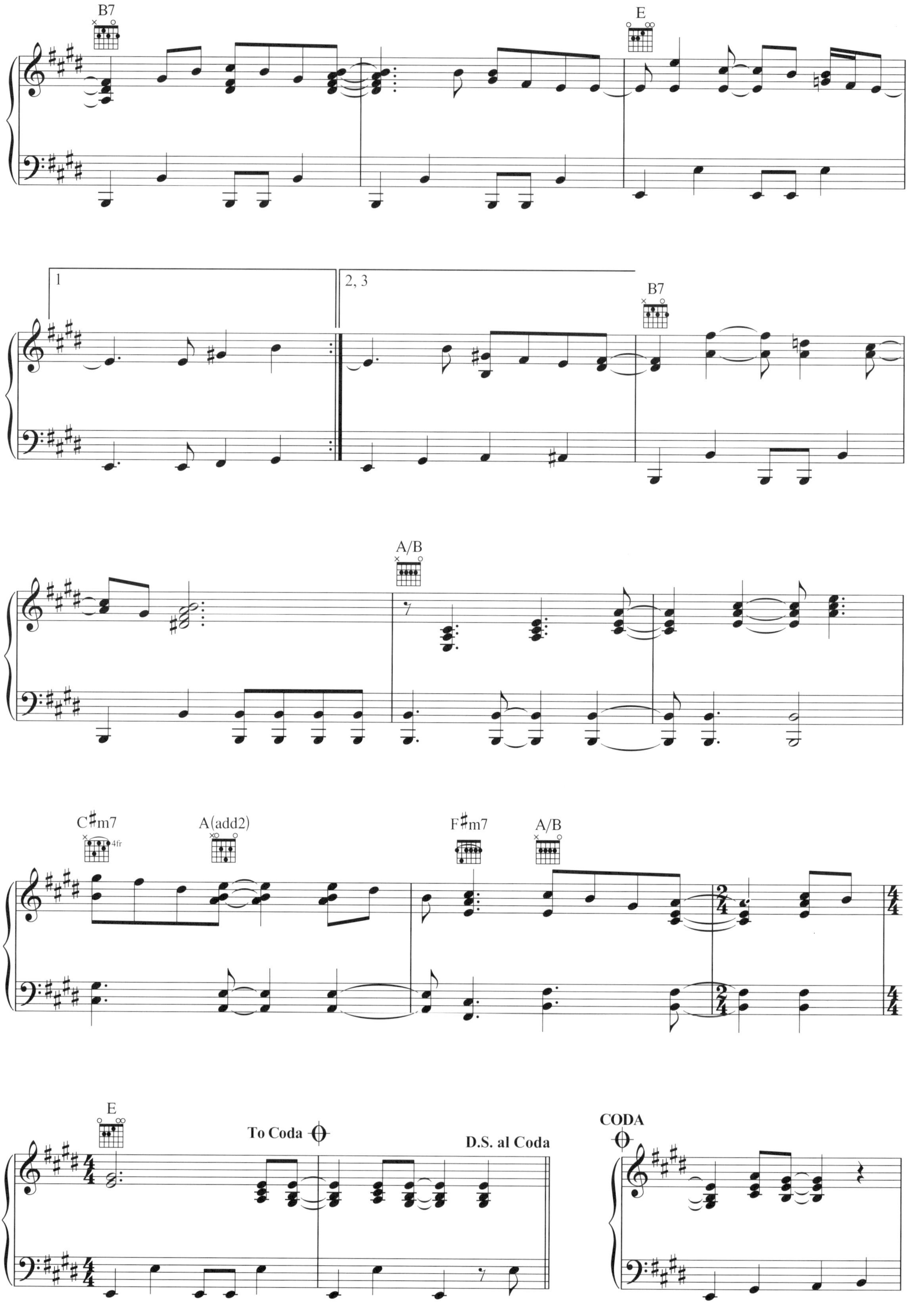
B7
E
1
2, 3
B7
A/B
C♯m7
4fr
A(add2)
F♯m7
A/B
E
To Coda
D.S. al Coda
CODA

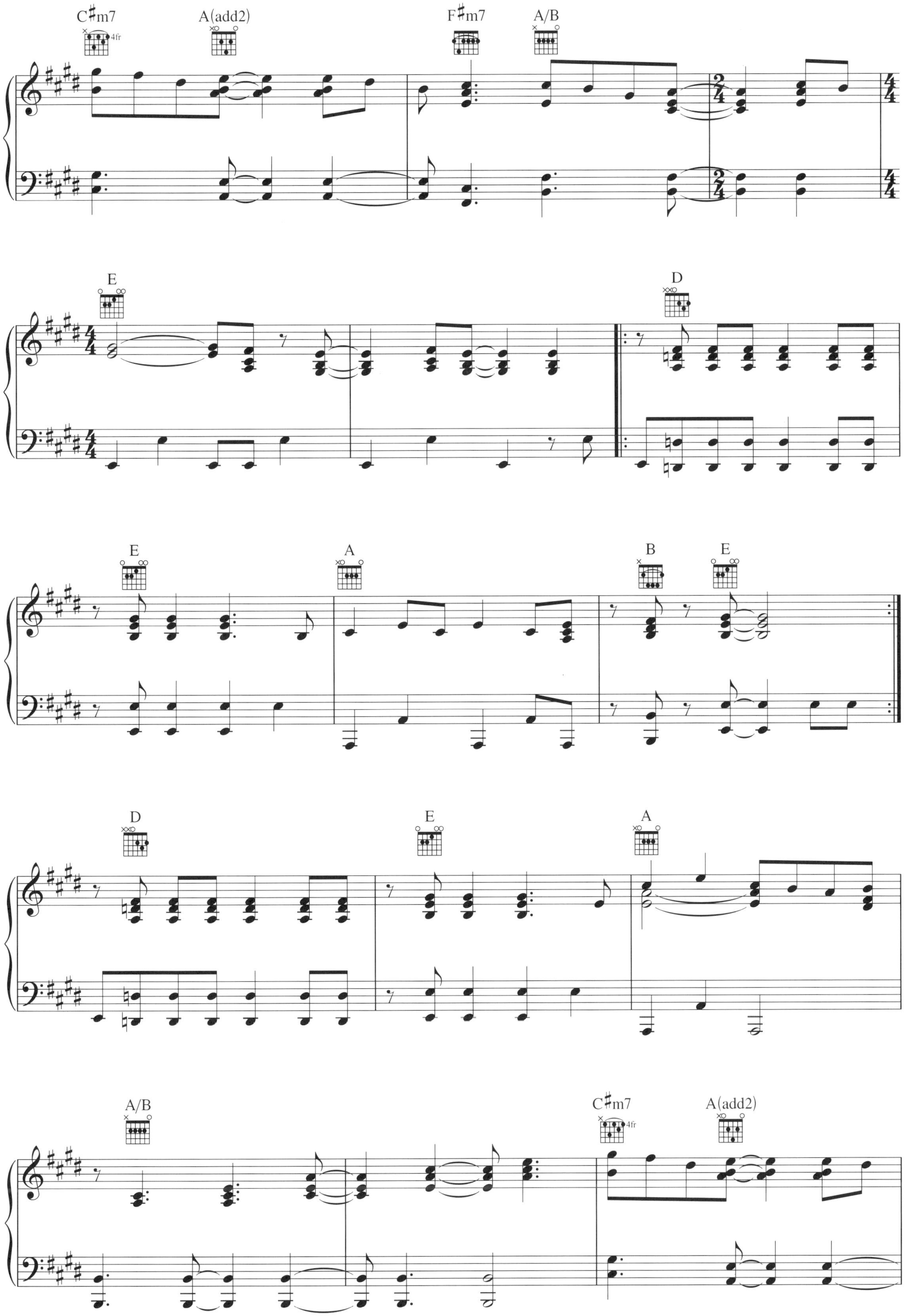

C♯m7
4fr
A(add2)
F♯m7
A/B
E
D
E
A
B
E
D
E
A
A/B
C♯m7
4fr
A(add2)

F♯m7
A/B
E
B7
E
Repeat and Fade
Optional Ending
B7
C♯m7
4fr
A(add2)
F♯m7
A/B
E
rit.

HEAR ME LORD

Words and Music by
GEORGE HARRISON

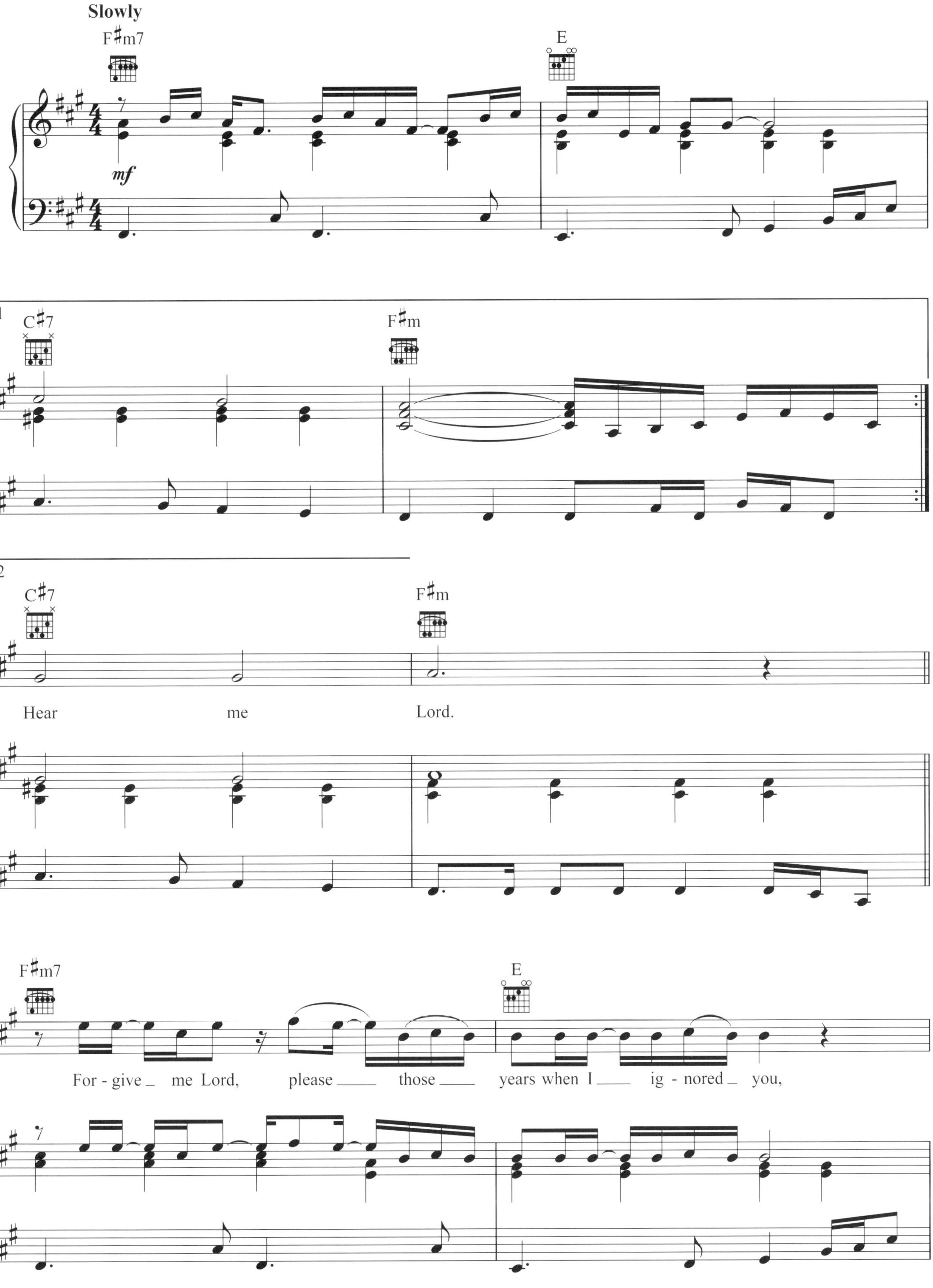

mmm.

Forgive them Lord those that feel they can't afford you,

mmm.

Help me Lord please, to rise above this dealing,

117

118

to the left and the right. Above and below us.

Out and in, there's no place that you're not in.

To Coda

Won't you hear me Lord?

(Ad lib. instrumental solo.)

119

C♯7
F♯m
D.S. al Coda
Hear me Lord.
CODA
E
C♯7
F♯m
Oh, won't you hear me Lord.
F♯m7
E
Help me Lord please, to rise a lit - tle high - er,
C♯7
F♯m
mmm.

Lyrics:

Help me Lord please, to burn out this desire,

mmm.

Hear me Lord, please, ooh.

(Lead vocal ad lib until end.) Ooh.

Hear me Lord, ooh.

123

HIS NAME IS LEGS
(Ladies and Gentlemen)

Words and Music by
GEORGE HARRISON

B7
Gm
3fr
Ev - 'ry - thing is dink - y do,
Peo - ple think he's loop - y loo,
G
D
A
ev - 'ry - thing you do.
and when they look at his shoes.
B7
You, the king of la di da.
He's a rock - ing sau - sage roll.
Gm
3fr
Vocal tacet on D.S.
G
D
Pret - ty ver - y out
He gets it in the

far.
goal.

Never over-sits, he under-stands
Healthy little brown af-fair

like the back of the hand.
and when he wash-es his hair.

He should sing in a band.
He'll get a round or a square.

C
1
G
Oh, yeah.
Get them
2, 3
G
F
G
sing - ing.
Both times: Ooh.
A
D
D/E
F
G
A
E
F
G
Ooh.

Ev-'ry-one from Ox-ford town, way
Coolies sweat-ing in Hong Kong run a-
down to the Ri-o Grande.
long to the Mar-di Grass.

Knows his har-bor quays, skin-tight hands,
Risking Asian flu to meet the man

who lays the eggs, / with-out segues, his name is Legs. his name is Legs.

D.S. al Coda

CODA

He's a cure for whoop-ing cough

and if the go-ing gets rough.

Get lined up, come Sikh, come Czar no mat-ter who you are.

131

We could get a-long and slide a rule and if you don't play fools while Lar-ry plays pool, you'll hear him sing-ing.

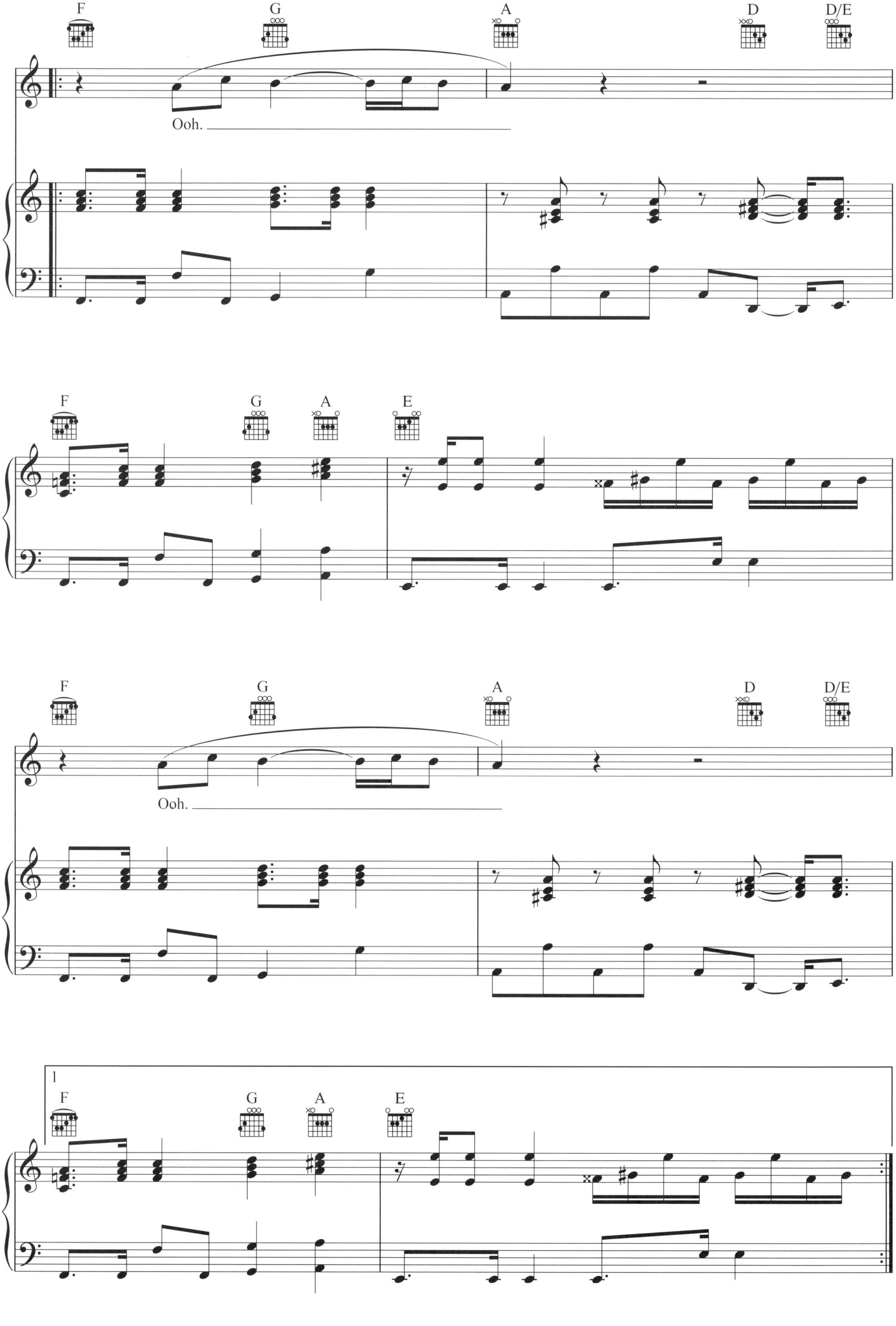
F G A D D/E
Ooh.
F G A E
F G A D D/E
Ooh.
1
F G A E

2
F
G
A
B7
Gm
3fr
G
D
A
B7
Repeat and Fade
Optional Ending
Gm
3fr
G
D
A

I DIG LOVE

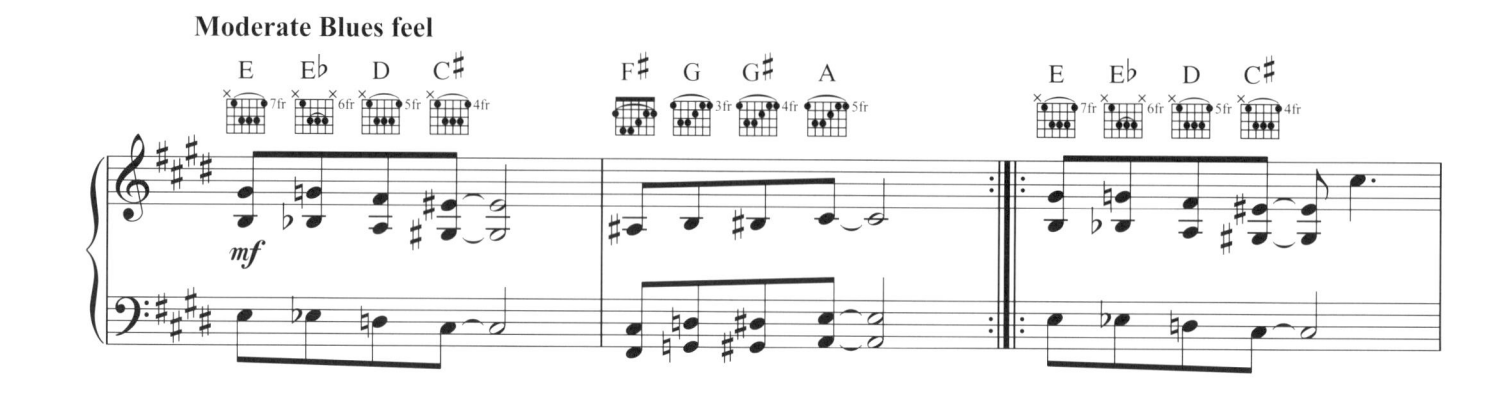

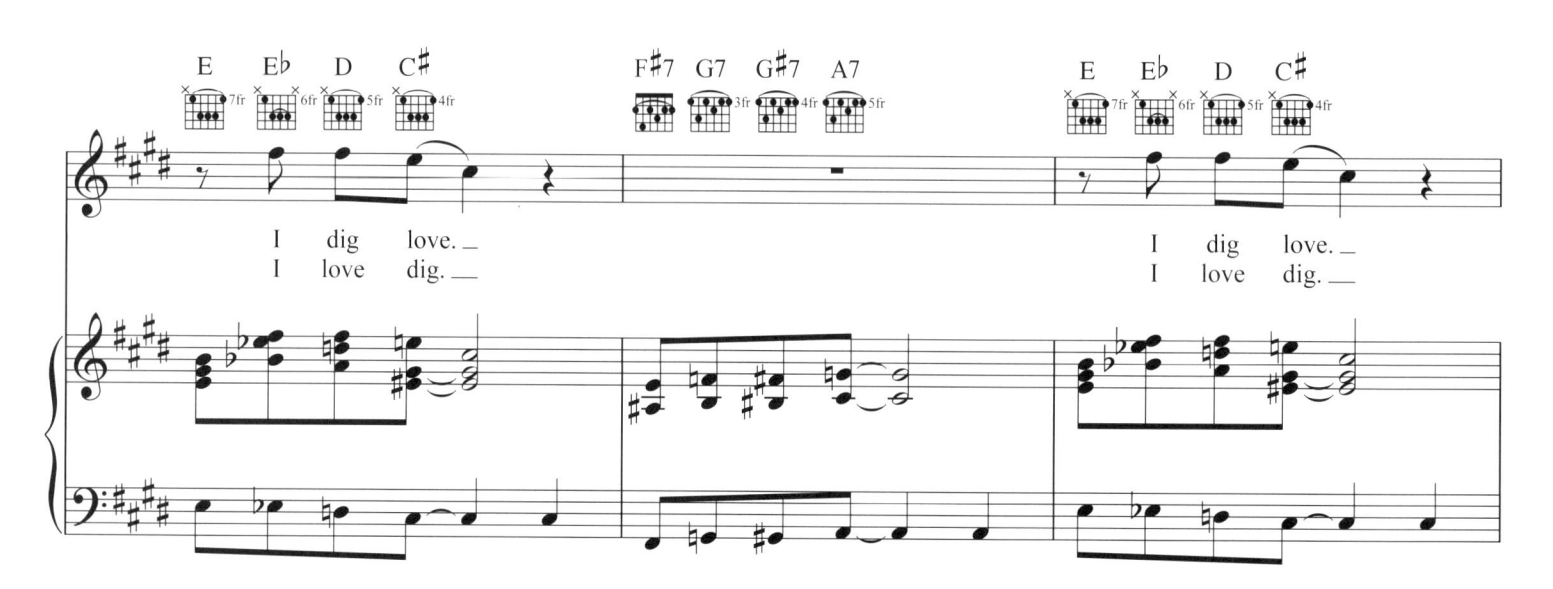

Words and Music by
GEORGE HARRISON

Moderate Blues feel

I dig love.
I love dig.

I dig love.
I love dig.

I dig love.
I love dig.

Copyright © 1970 Harrisongs Ltd.
Copyright Renewed
All Rights Reserved

F♯7 G7 G♯7 A7
E
E7
Mmmm, I dig love in the morn - in'.
Mmmm, I love dig in the morn - in'.
A
A♯dim
E
C♯7
I dig love in the eve - nin'.
I love dig ev - 'ry eve - nin'.
I dig love and I
F♯7 G7 G♯7 A7
want you to know I dig love.
1
E E♭ D C♯
F♯7 G7 G♯7 A7
E E♭ D C♯
F♯7 G7 G♯7 A7
Mmm,
2
E E♭ D C♯

F♯7 G7 G♯7 A7
G♯7
C♯m
3fr 4fr 5fr 4fr
Mmm, small love, big love, I don't care. Love's all
Bought love, short love, in an - y port, love's al -
B7
E7
G♯7
good love to me. Left love, right love,
- ways there to see. Make love, take love but
C♯m
F♯7
C7
B7
an - y - where love, There's a rare love, come on and get it, it's free.
you should give love. Try to live love. Come on, that's where you should be.
E E♭ D C♯
F♯7 G7 G♯7 A7
E E♭ D C♯
7fr 6fr 5fr 4fr
I dig love.
I dig love.

F♯7 G7 G♯7 A7
E E♭ D C♯
F♯7 G7 G♯7 A7
I dig love. Mmm,
E
E7
A
I dig love in the morn - in'. I dig love
A♯dim
E
C♯7
F♯7 G7 G♯7 A7
To Coda
in the eve - nin'. I dig love and I want you to know I dig love.
E7 E♭7 D7 C♯7
F♯7 G7 G♯7 A7
E7 E♭7 D7 C♯7

138

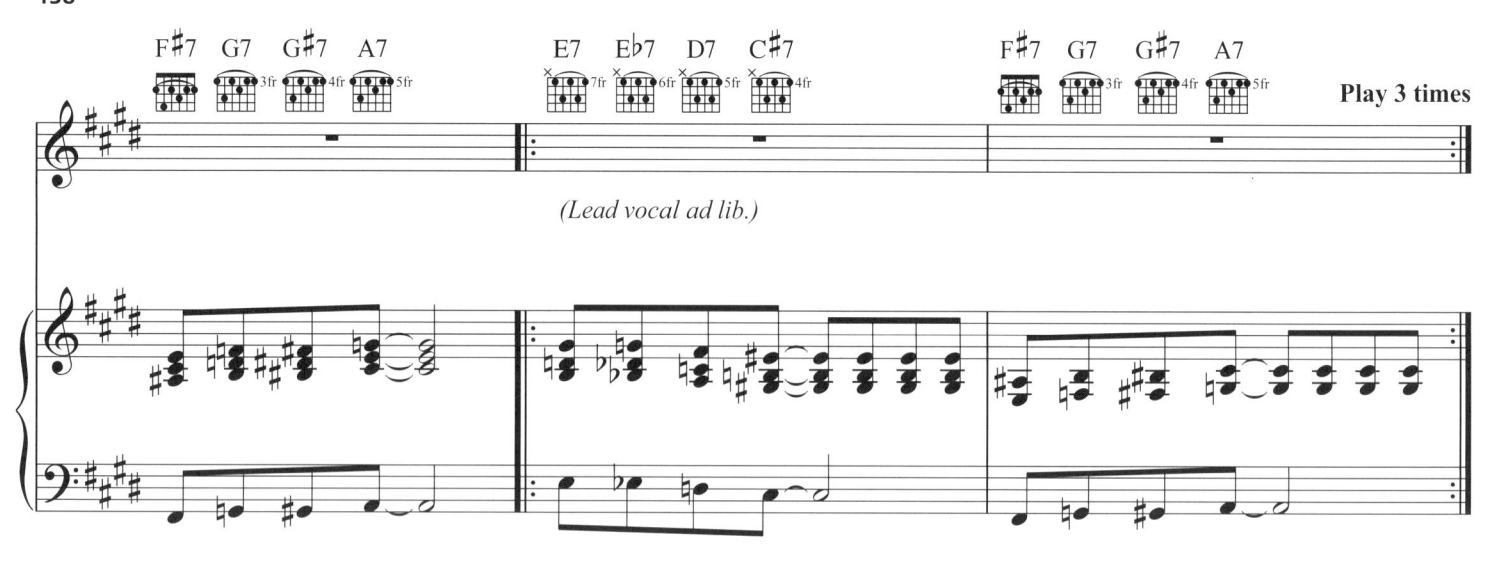

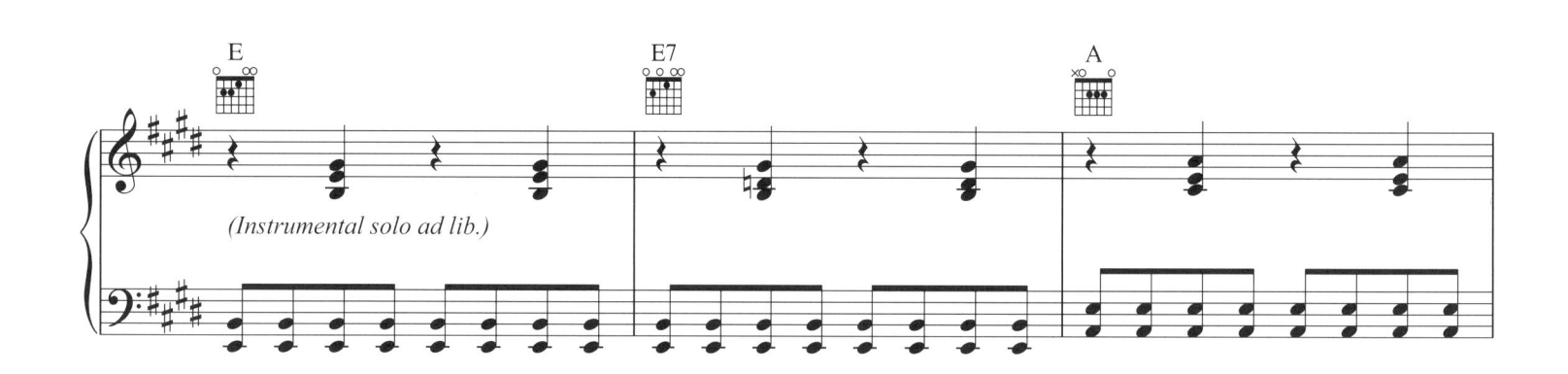

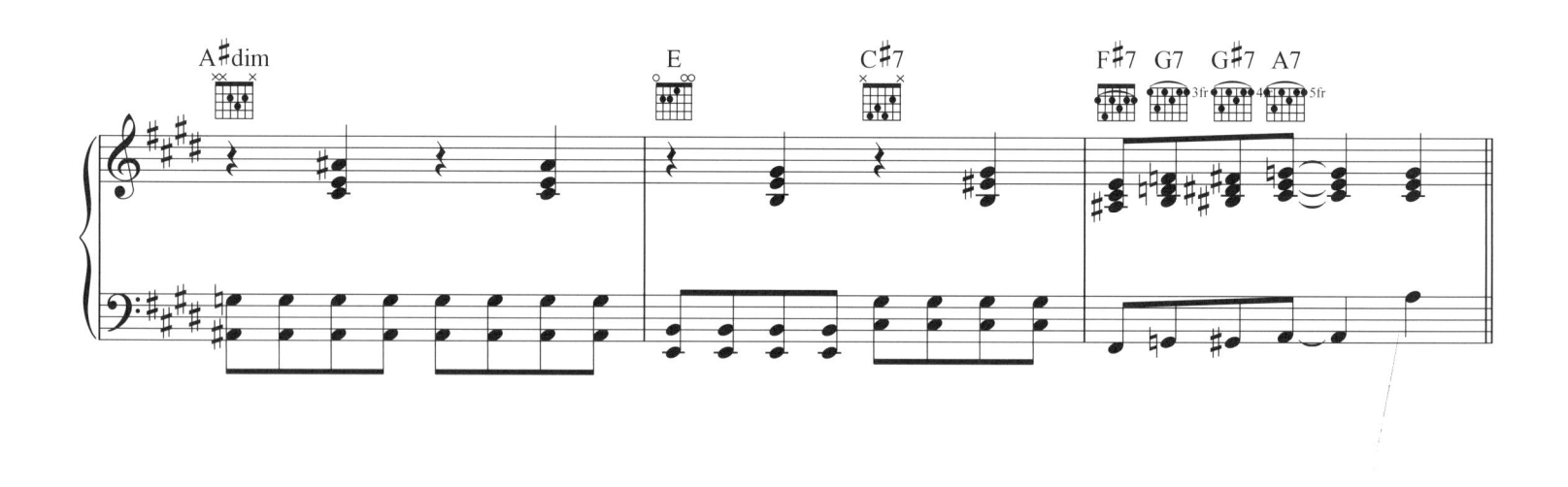

F♯7 G7 G♯7 A7
D.S. al Coda
CODA
E C♯7
Yes, I want
F♯7 A7 E C♯7 F♯7 A7
you to know I dig love. Yes, I want you to know I dig
E C♯7 F♯7 G7 G♯7 A7
love.
Repeat and Fade
E E♭ D C♯
(Lead vocal ad lib.)
F♯7 G7 G♯7 A7
Optional Ending
E

I DON'T CARE ANYMORE

Words and Music by
GEORGE HARRISON

Moderately

Play 3 times

I don't care anymore,
If your man should get up tight,
it can't be so bad, be-

*Recorded a half step higher.

Copyright © 1974 Umlaut Corporation
Copyright Renewed
All Rights Reserved

and I'll kick down an-y-bod-y's door
cause you've been a-lone for most the night,
what you want that you've not had.

to hold you in my arms once more.
now re-al-ize your need's al-right,
It's like-ly to up-set your dad.

I'd
then
I don't

go an-y-where, you know, I don't
get back up them stairs, you know, I don't
think that it's un-fair, you know, I don't

142

care.
care.
care

Oh, there's a line that I can draw,

143

with you. Now an-y-more. But I'd kick down an-y-bod-y's door to hold you in my arms once more. I'd go an-y-where, you know, well, I...

Repeat and Fade

Optional Ending

I LIVE FOR YOU

Words and Music by
GEORGE HARRISON

Moderate Country

All a-lone ___ in ___ this world ___ am I. ___ Not a care ___ for ___ this world ___ have I. ___
Not a thing ___ in ___ this world ___ do I own. ___ On-ly sad-ness ___ from all ___ that is grown. ___

*Recorded a half step higher.

Copyright © 2000 Harrisongs Ltd.
All Rights Reserved

C
Em
On - ly you keep my eyes
In this dark - ness I wait
Am
C
op - en wide.
for the day.
G
Yes it's true,
Yes it's true,
Am
C
I live for you.
I live for you.

Am
Dm
C
Am
For man - y years
I wait.
Dm
C
Am
Dm
Through man - y tears
I wait.

149

150

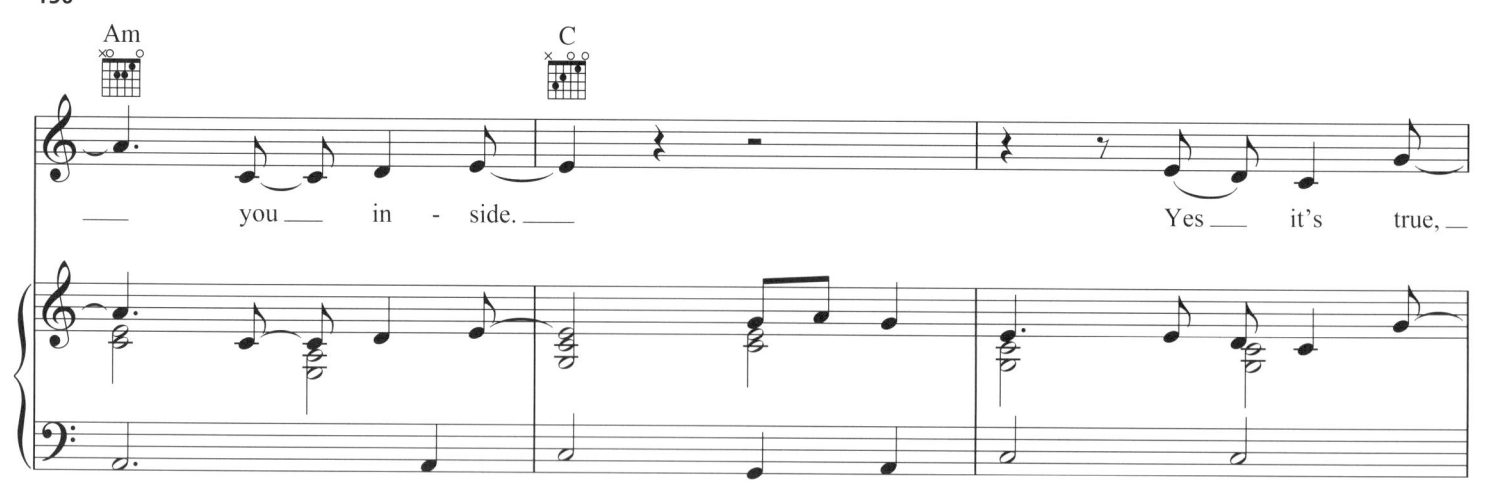

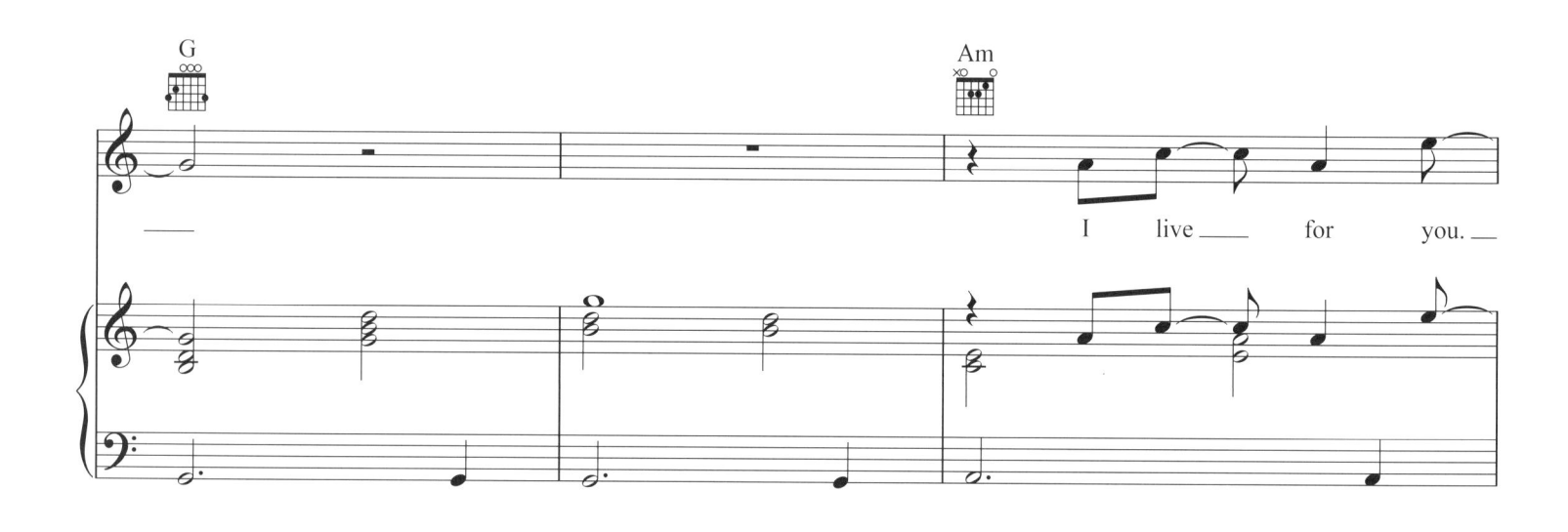

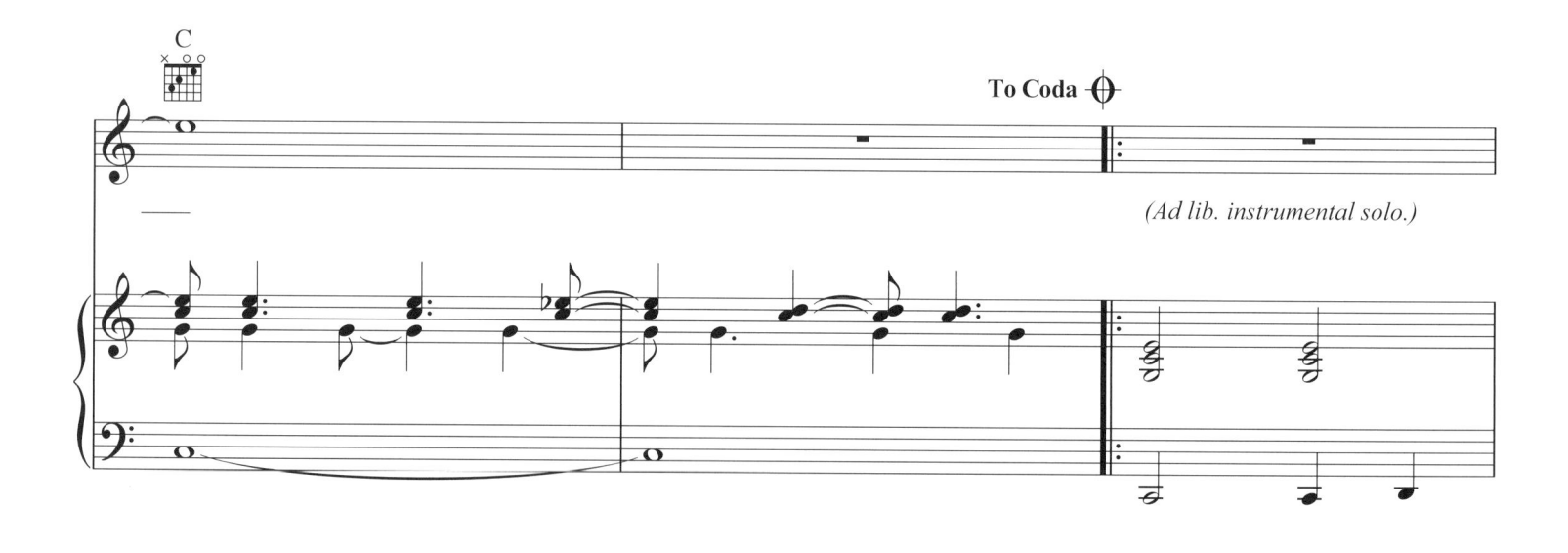

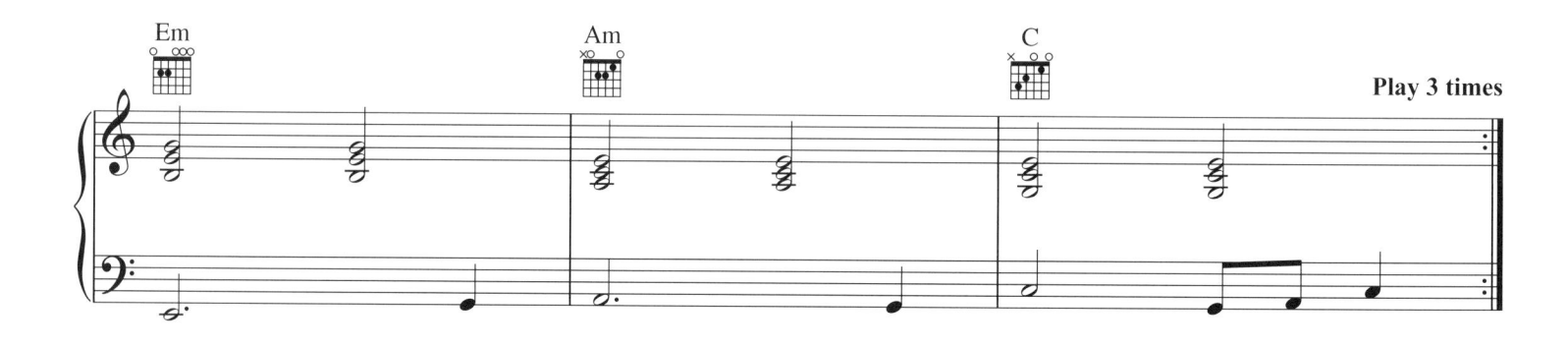

151

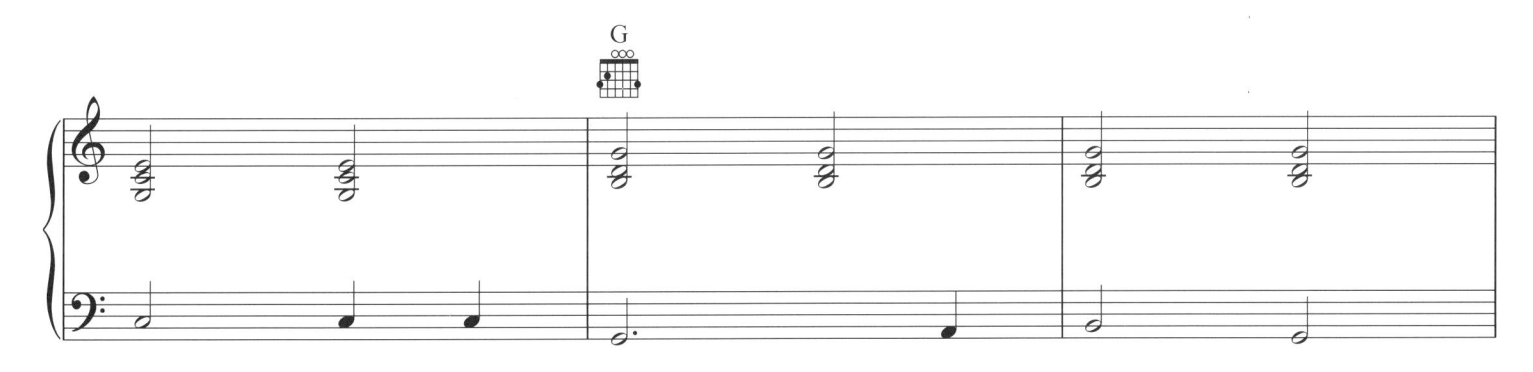

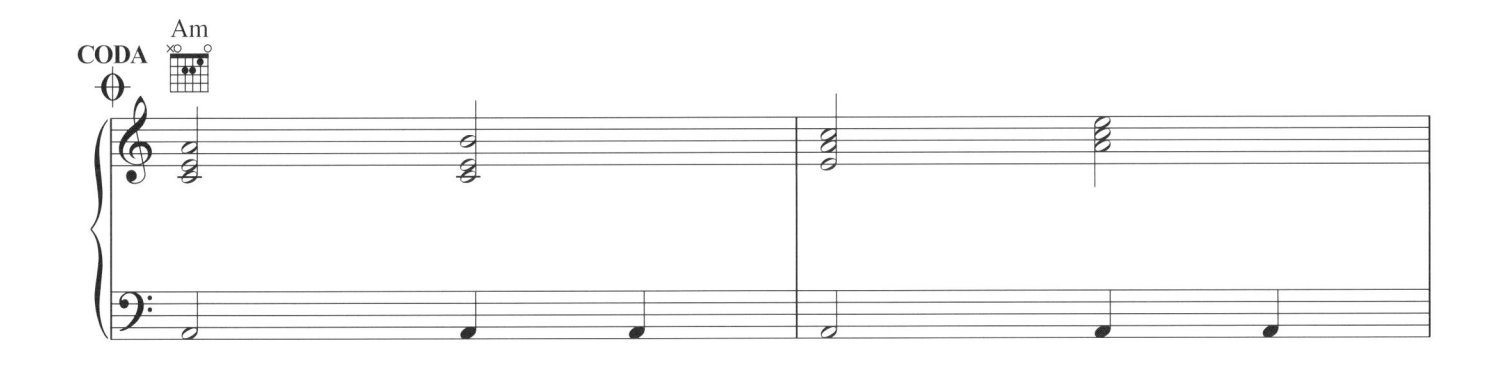

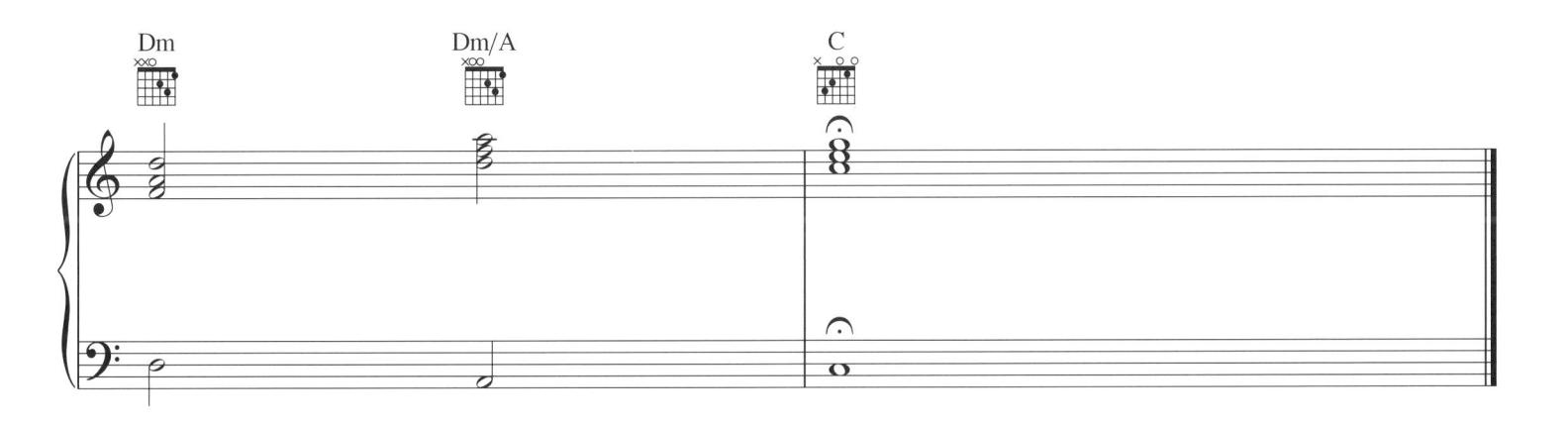

I'D HAVE YOU ANY TIME

Words and Music by GEORGE HARRISON
and BOB DYLAN

Let me show ___ you. Let me roll it to
Let me show ___ you. Let me grow up — on

you.
you.

All I have is yours.

All you see is ___ mine. ___ And I'm

154

IF NOT FOR YOU

Words and Music by
BOB DYLAN

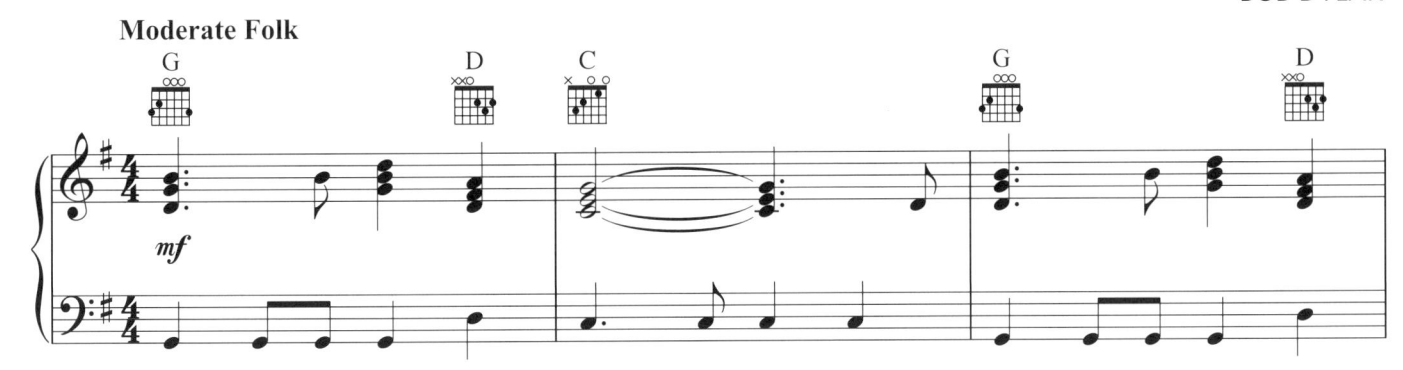

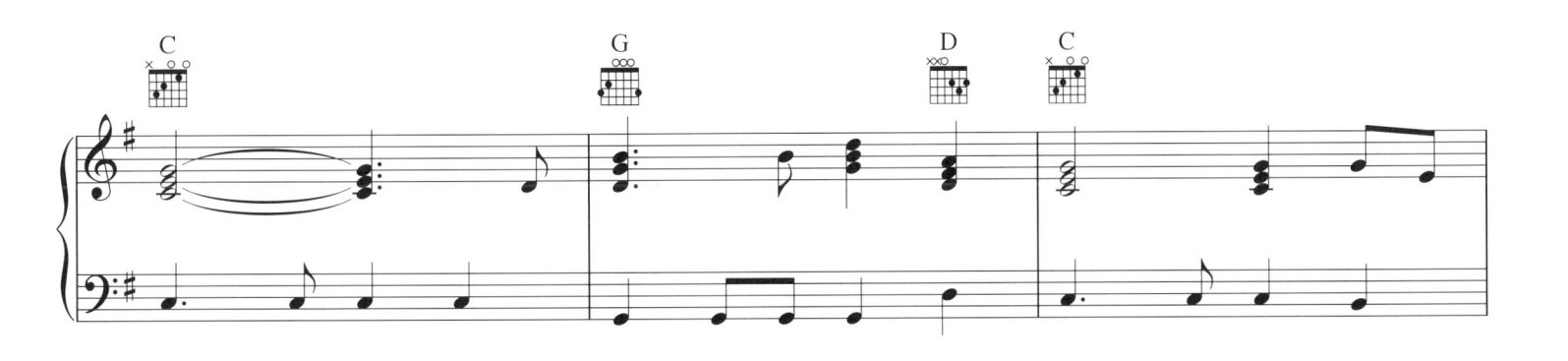

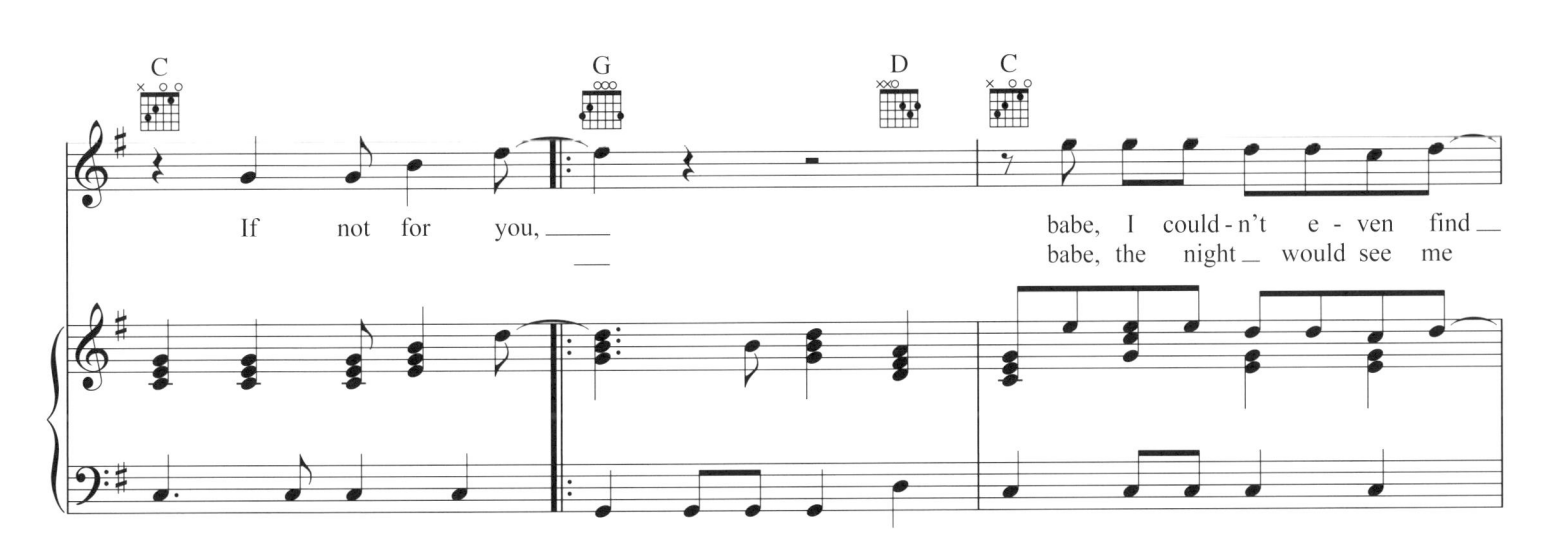

Moderate Folk

If not for you, _____ babe, I could-n't e-ven find _____
_____ babe, the night _____ would see me

Copyright © 1970, 1985 Big Sky Music
International Copyright Secured   All Rights Reserved
Used by Permission

156

would fall, rain would gather too.

With-out your love I'd be no - where at all. I'd be lost if not for you.

If not for you, the win - ter would hold

no spring. Could-n't hear the rob-in sing.

I just would-n't have a clue, if not for you.

(Ad lib. harmonica solo)

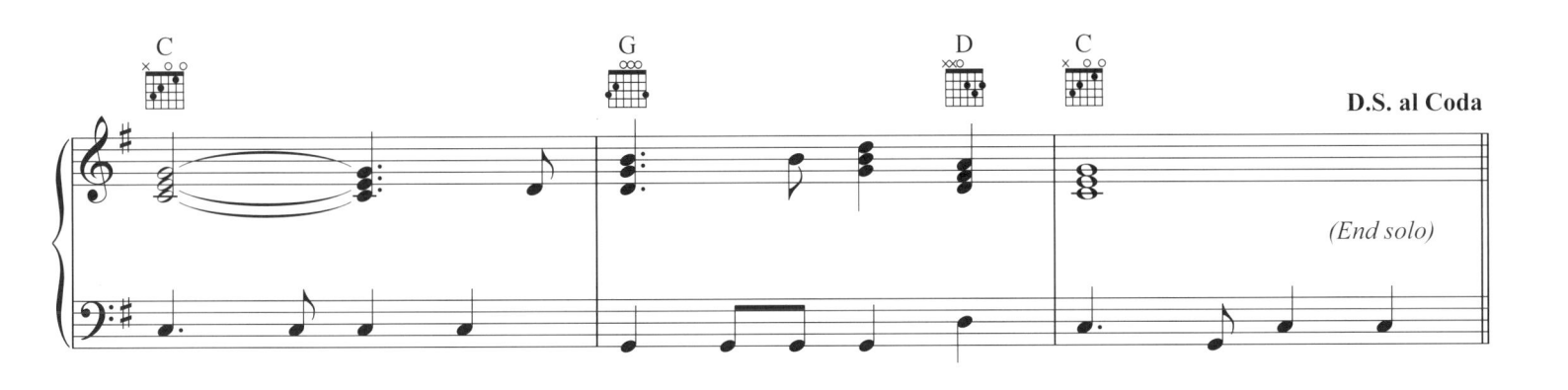

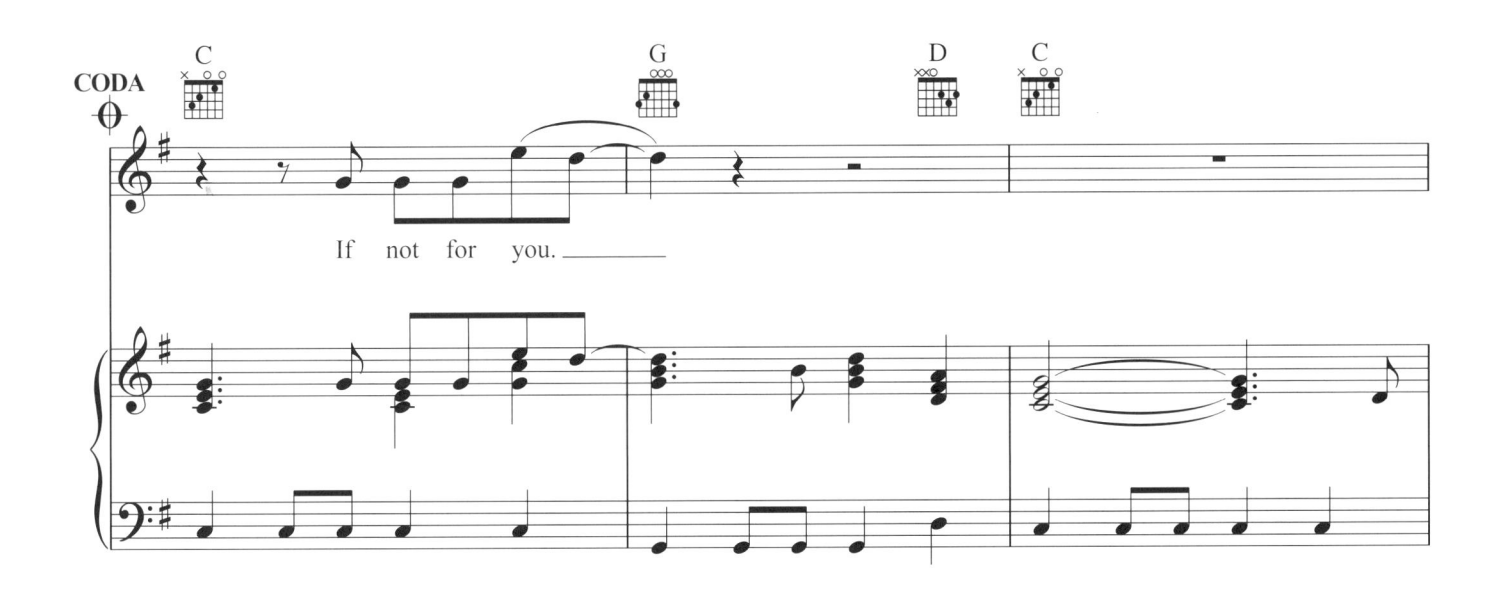

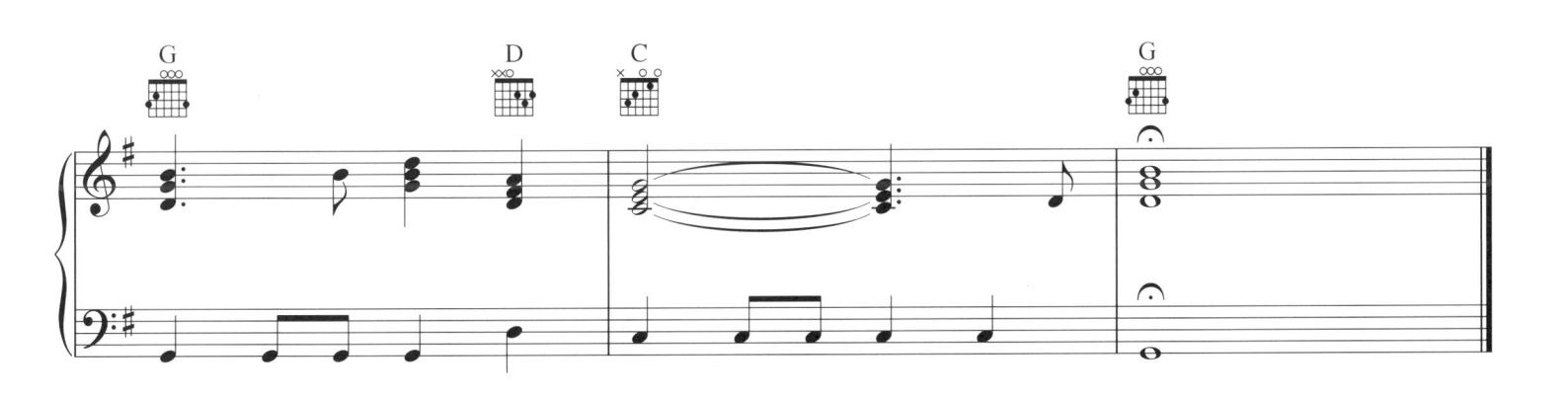

If not for you.

ISN'T IT A PITY

Words and Music by
GEORGE HARRISON

Moderately slow

Is-n't it a pit-y? Now is-n't it a shame how we break each oth-er's hearts and cause each oth-er pain; how we take each oth-er's

Copyright © 1970 Harrisongs Ltd.
Copyright Renewed 1998
All Rights Reserved

love　　with-out think-ing an - y - more, for - get-ting to give back.＿　Isn't it a pit - y?＿　Some things take so long,＿ but how do I ex - plain　　when not too man - y peo - ple can see we're all the same?

And be-cause of all their tears, their eyes can't hope to see the beau - ty that sur - rounds them.

Is-n't it a pit-y?

Forgetting to give back,_____ isn't it a

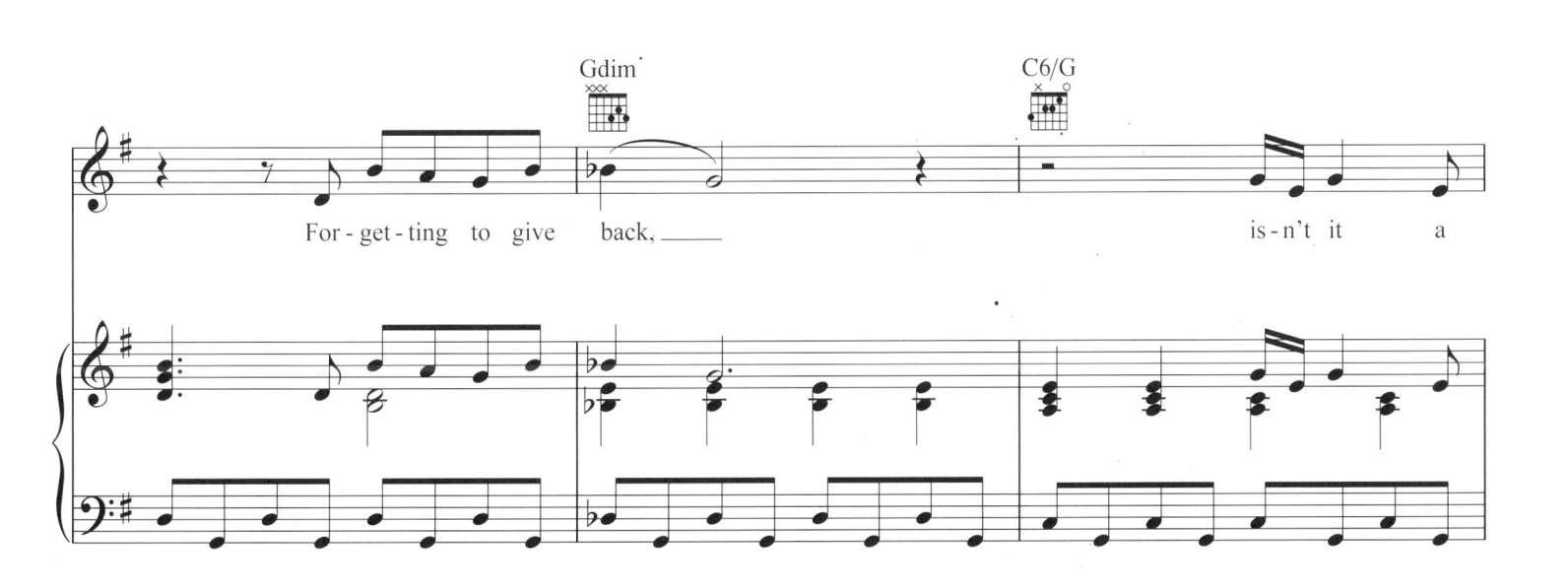

pit-y?

For-get-ting to give back, now, is-n't it a pit-y?

Repeat and Fade

IT'S JOHNNY'S BIRTHDAY

Words and Music by BILL MARTIN
and PHIL COULTER

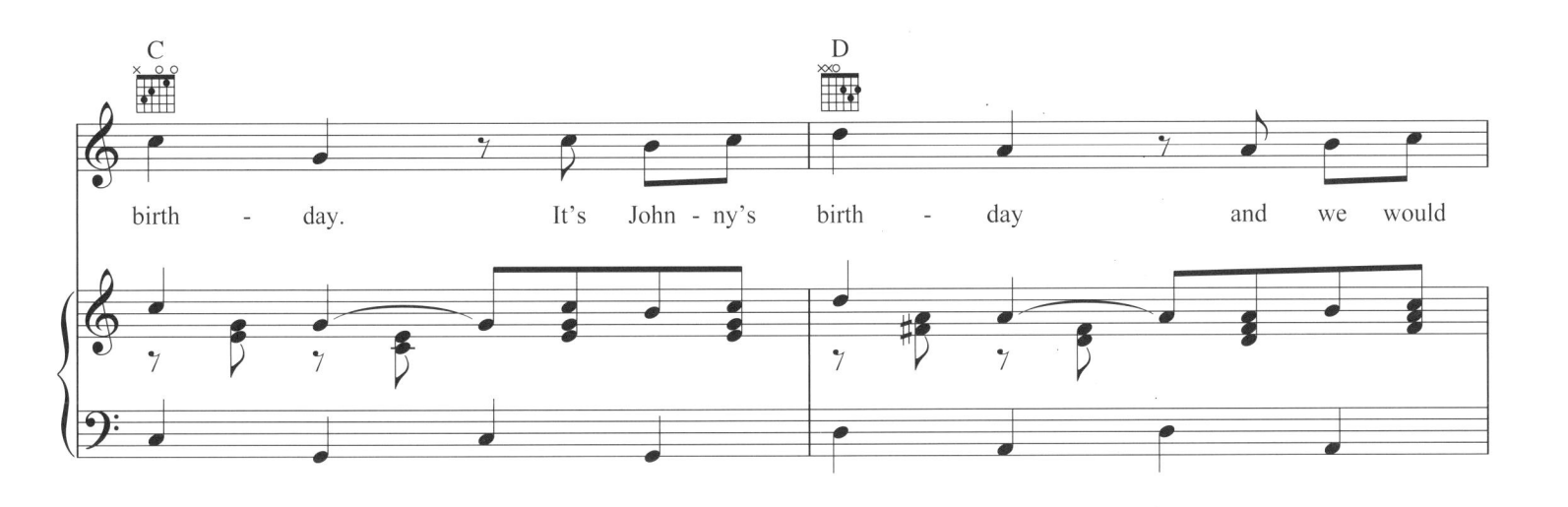

Moderate Circus feel

It's John-ny's birth-day. It's John-ny's birth-day and we would like to wish him all the ver-y best. It's John-ny's

---

* Recorded a half step lower. Recording varies in speed and pitch but is written as it was recorded before the effect was added.

© 1970 (Renewed) EMI AL GALLICO MUSIC CORP. on behalf of Peter Maurice Music Co. LTD.
Exclusive Print Rights for EMI AL GALLICO MUSIC CORP. Administered by ALFRED MUSIC
All Rights Reserved   Used by Permission

birth - day. It's John - ny's birth - day. And it's so nice to have you back, so be our guest at John - ny's birth - day, at John - ny's birth - day. We'd like to wish you all what we would wish our -

E♭
3fr
selves. On John - ny's birth - day, it's John - ny's
F
B♭
birth - day. And it's so good to have you back a - mongst the
E♭
3fr
F
shelves. And it's so good to have you
B♭
E♭
3fr
back a - mongst the shelves.

IT IS "HE"
(Jai Sri Krishna)

Words and Music by
GEORGE HARRISON

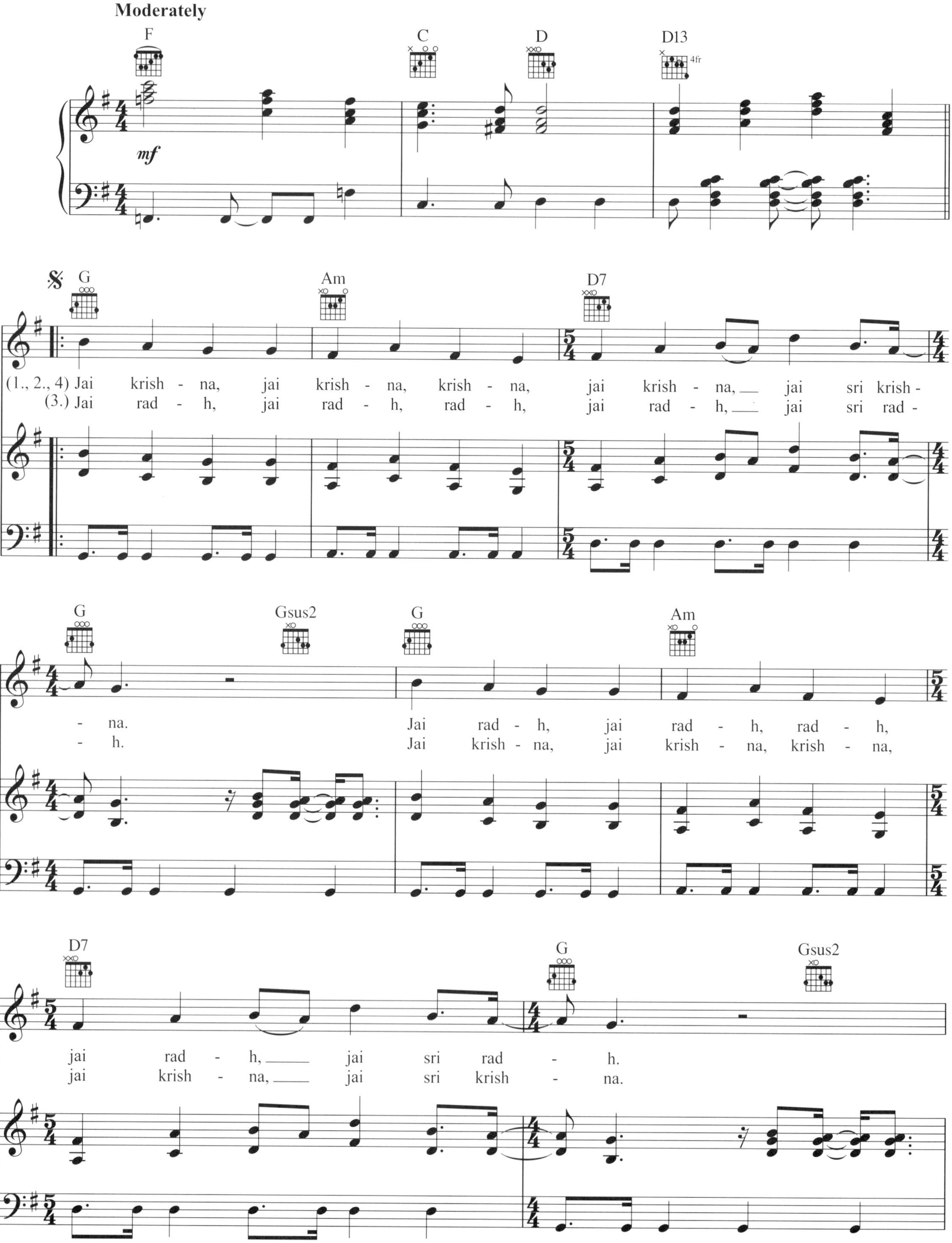

Jai krish-na, jai krish-na, krish-na, jai krish-na, jai sri krish-na. Jai radh, jai
Jai radh, jai radh, radh, jai radh, jai sri radh. Jai krish-na, jai

radh, radh, jai radh, jai sri radh.
krish-na, krish-na, jai krish-na, jai sri krish-na.

(1.) He whose eyes have seen
(2.) He whose sweet-ness flows
(3.) He who is com-plete,

what our lives have been,
to any one of those
three worlds at his feet,

who we really are,
that cares to look his way,
cause of ev-'ry star,

it is "he," jai sri krishna.
see his smile, jai sri radh.
it is "he,"

jai sri krishna.

D.S. al Coda

CODA
G Gsus2 G Am
h. Jai krish - na, jai krish - na, krish - na,
D7 G Gsus2 G
jai krish - na, jai sri krish - na. Jai rad - h, jai
Am
rad - h, rad - h,
Repeat and Fade
D7 G Gsus2
jai rad - h, jai sri rad - h.
Optional Ending
D7 G
jai rad - h, jai sri rad - h.

LET IT DOWN

Words and Music by
GEORGE HARRISON

Though you sit in an-oth-er chair,
While I oc-cu-py my mind,
While you look so sweet-ly and di-vine,

I can feel you here.
I can feel you here.
I can feel you here.

Copyright © 1970 Harrisongs Ltd.
Copyright Renewed 1998
All Rights Reserved

Looking like I don't care,
Love to us is so well-timed,
I see your eyes are busy kissing mine,

but I do, I do.
and I do, I do.
and I do, I do.

Hiding it all behind
Wasting away these mo-
Wondering what it is

anything I see,
-ments so heavenly,
they're expecting to see,

should someone be look-
should someone be look-
should someone be look-

1
E7
Emaj7
- ing at me.
mp
Amaj7
2, 3
E7
- ing at me.
E
Let it down.
f
E7
Let it down.
F♯7/E
Let your hair

Fmaj7/E
E7
hang all a - round me.
E
E7
Let it down.
Let it all
down.
F#7/E
Fmaj7/E
To Coda
Let your love flow and as - tound
E7
Emaj7
me.

Amaj7
D.S. al Coda
CODA
E7
me.
E
Let it down.
Let it down.
F♯7/E
Whoa,
Fmaj7/E
whoa,
Repeat and Fade
E7
whoa.
Optional Ending
E7
whoa.

THE LIGHT THAT HAS LIGHTED THE WORLD

Words and Music by
GEORGE HARRISON

Slowly (half-time feel)

I've heard how some people have said that I've
funny how people just won't accept

changed, that I'm not what I was, how it
change, as if nature itself they'd pre-

realy is a shame. The
fer re-arranged. So

Copyright © 1973 The Material World Charitable Foundation Ltd. and Harrisongs Ltd.
Copyright Renewed
All Rights Reserved

| G | Bm/F# | Em7 |

thoughts in their heads man-i-fest on their brow,
hard to move on when you're down in a hole,

| G/D | A9 |

like bad scars from ill feel-ings they
where there's so lit-tle chance to ex-

| Am7 | Am9 | D13 |

them-selves a-rouse. So
per-i-ence soul. I'm

| Am | E♭dim7 | G |

hate-ful of an-y-one that is hap-py or free,
grate-ful to an-y-one that is hap-py or free

they live all their lives with - out
for - giv - ing me hope while I'm

look - ing to see
look - ing to see } the light that has light -

- ed the world.

Instrumental solo

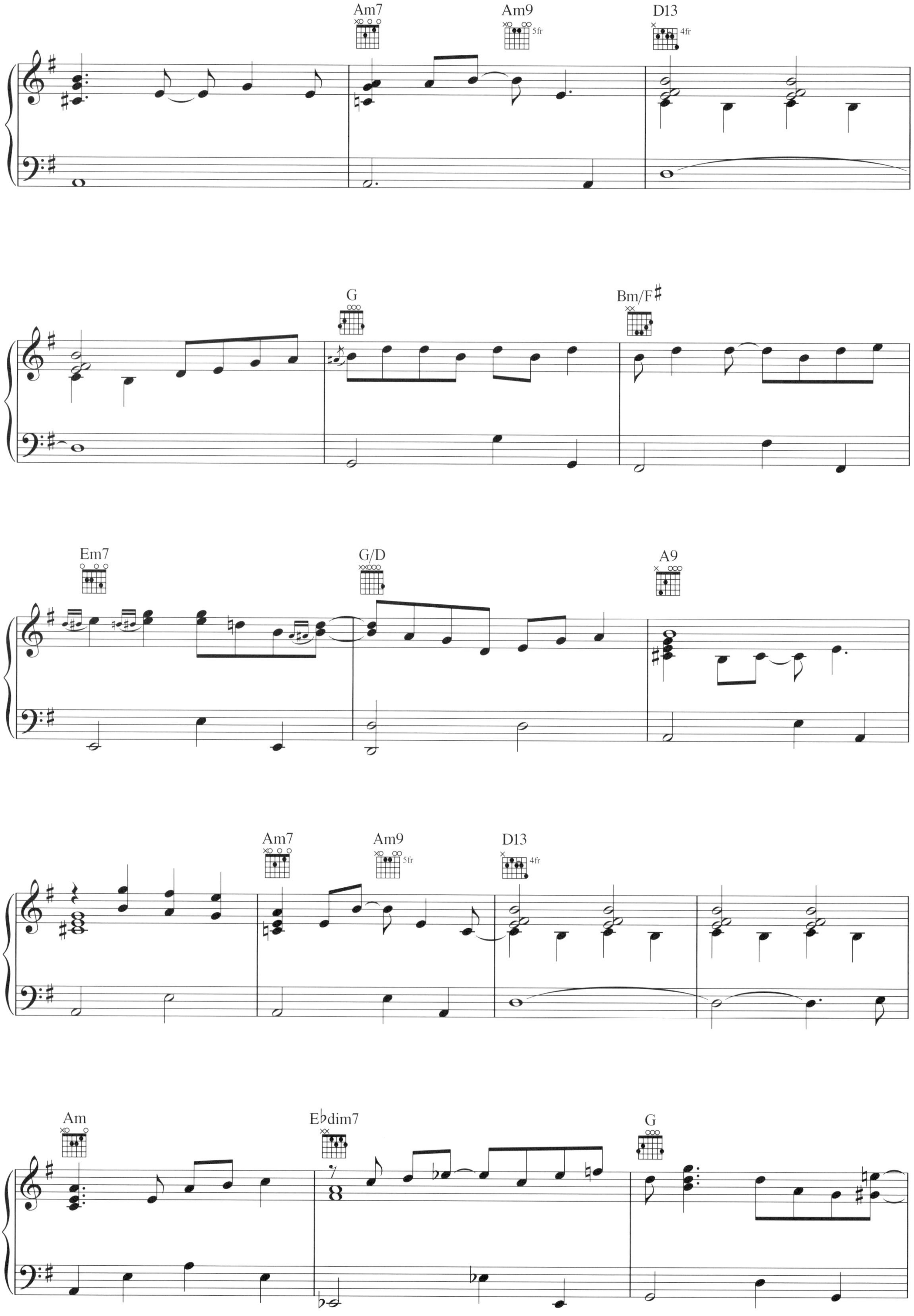
Am7
Am9
5fr
D13
4fr
G
Bm/F♯
Em7
G/D
A9
Am7
Am9
5fr
D13
4fr
Am
E♭dim7
G

Solo ends It's

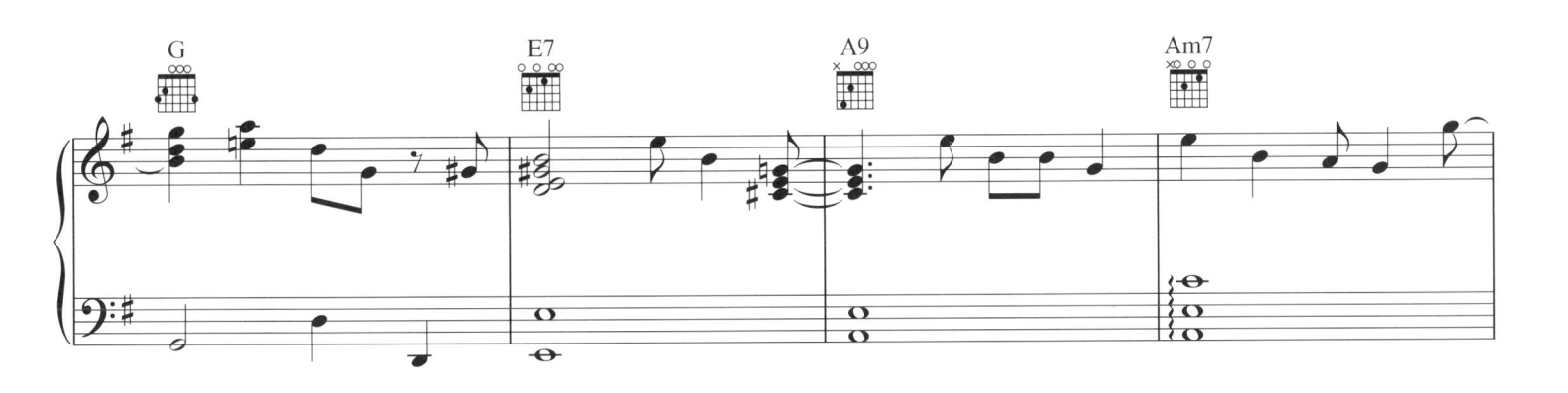

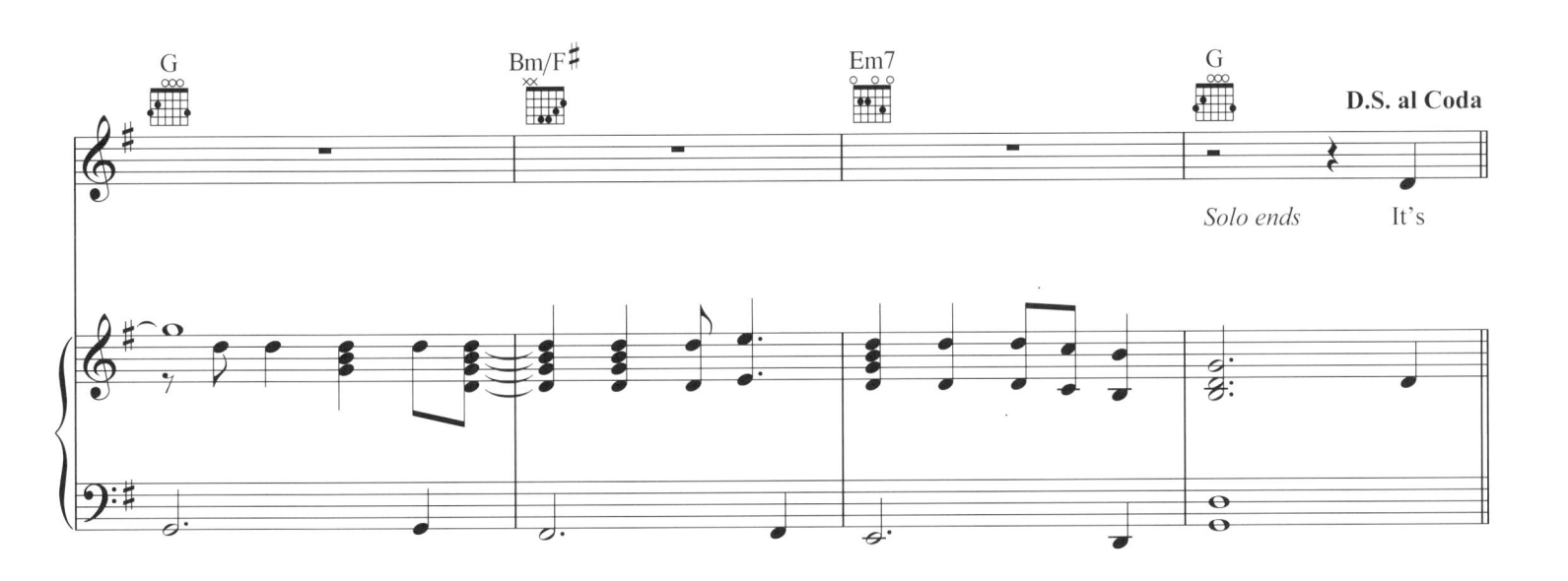

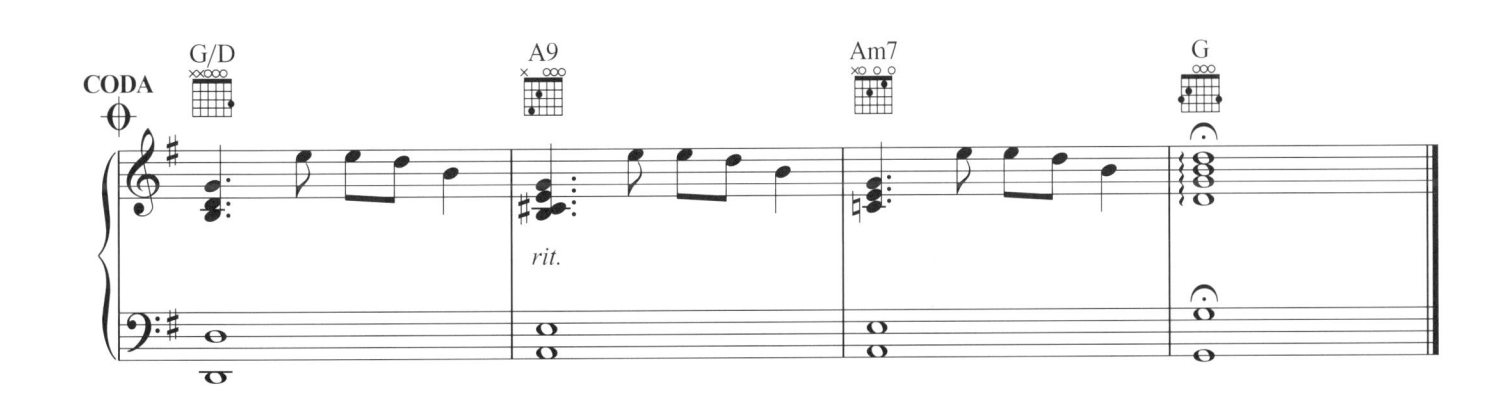

LIVING IN THE MATERIAL WORLD

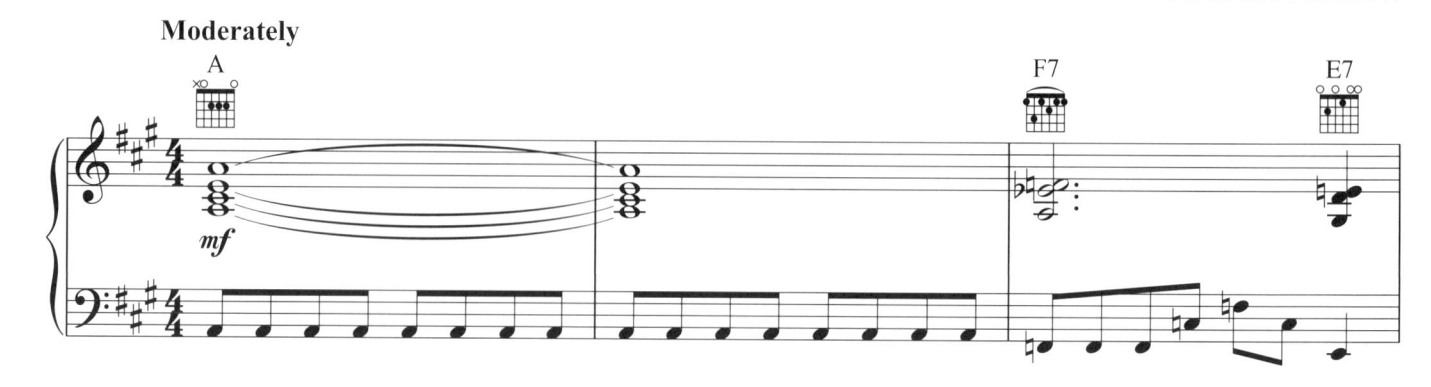

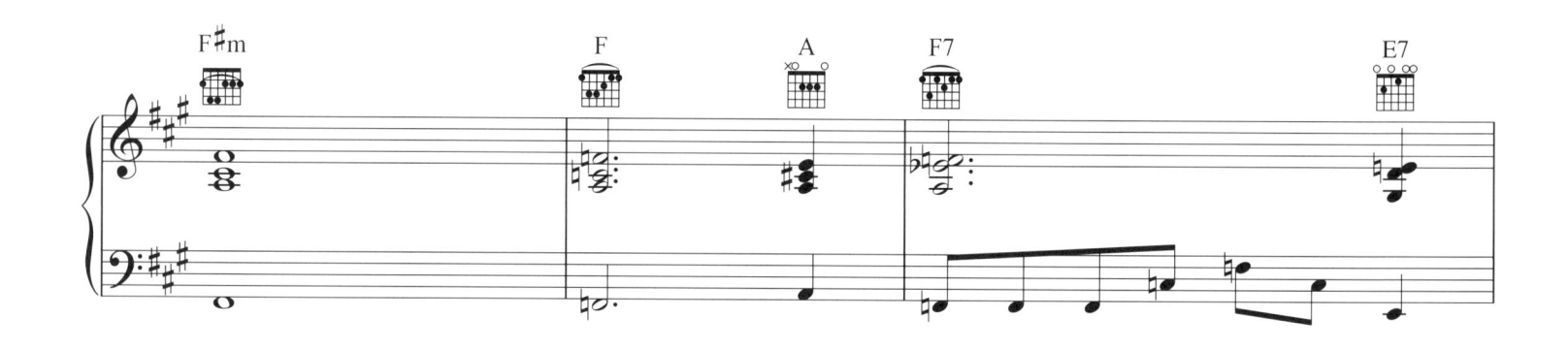

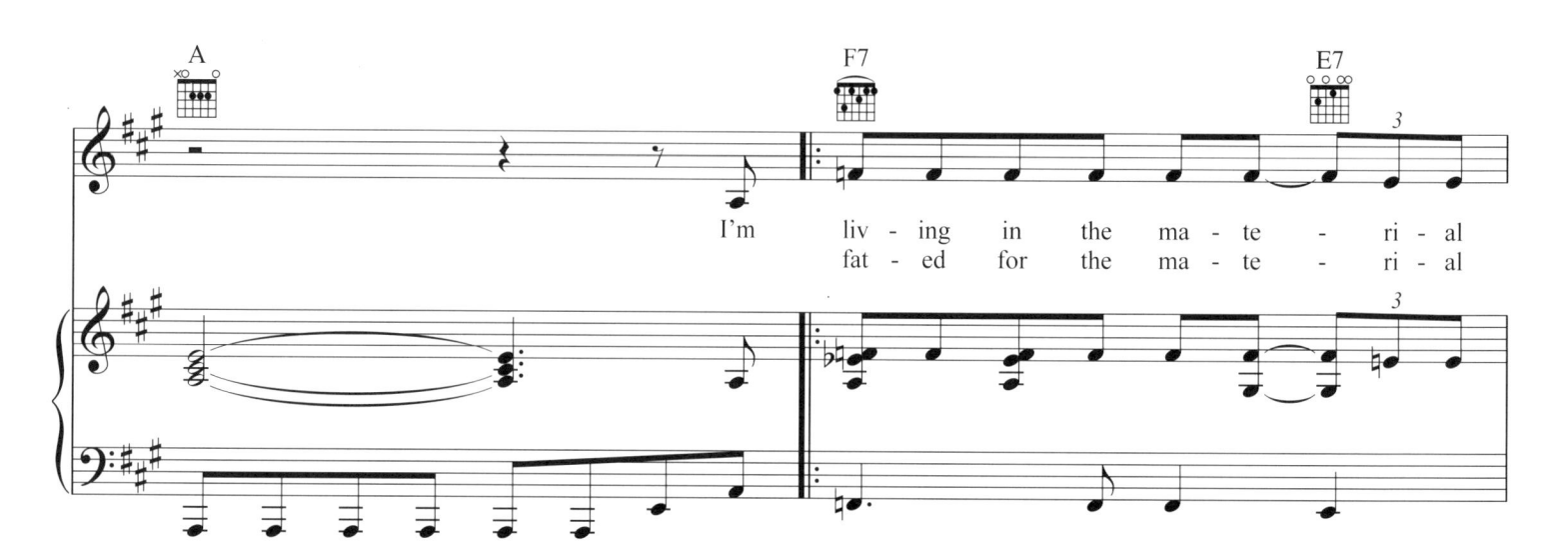

Words and Music by
GEORGE HARRISON

Moderately

I'm living in the ma-te-rial
fat-ed for the ma-te-rial

Copyright © 1973 The Material World Charitable Foundation Ltd.
Copyright Renewed
All Rights Reserved

world, _____ living in the mate - ri - al
world, _____ get frus - trat - ed in the mate - ri - al

world. Can't say what I'm do - ing here, __ but I
world. Sens - es nev - er grat - i - fied, __ on - ly

hope to see __ much clear - er af - ter living in the mate - ri - al
swell - ing like __ a tide that could drown me in the mate - ri - al

world. _____ I got born __
world. _____ *(Instrumental)*

(D.S.) _____ in - to the ma - te - ri - al world; _____ get - ting worn
(D.S.) liv - ing in the ma - te - ri - al world, _____ not much giv -

_____ out in the ma - te - ri - al world. Use my
- ing in the ma - te - ri - al world. Got a

bod - y like a car, _____ tak - ing me both near and far. Met my
lot of work to do; _____ try to get a mes - sage through. Get back

friends all in the ma - te - ri - al world. _____
out of this ma - te - ri - al world. _____

Met them all here in the material
I'm living in the material
world, John and Paul here in the material
world, living in the material
world. Though we started out quite poor, we got
world. I hope to
"rich-ie" on a tour. Got caught

up in the ma-te-ri-al ___ world. ___

(Instrumental ends)

From the Spir-it-u-al Sky, such sweet ___ mem-m'ries ___ have ___ I.

187

my sal - va - tion from the ma - te - ri - al world.

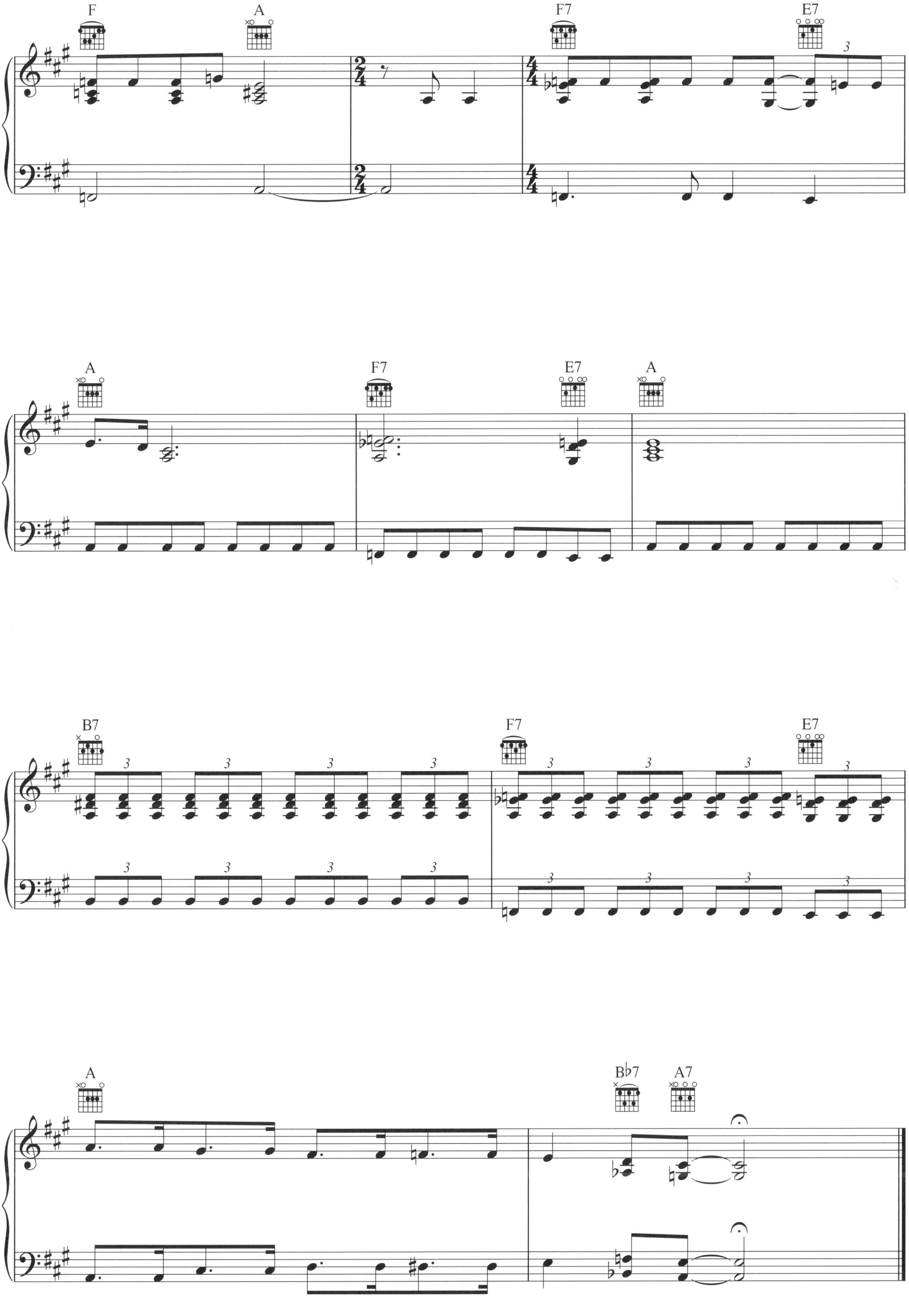
F
A
F7
E7
A
F7
E7
A
B7
F7
E7
A
B♭7
A7

THE LORD LOVES THE ONE
(That Loves the Lord)

Words and Music by
GEORGE HARRISON

*Recorded a whole step higher.

Copyright © 1973 The Material World Charitable Foundation Ltd. and Harrisongs Ltd.
Copyright Renewed
All Rights Reserved

E7
A7
give, then you don't get lov - in'.
Now, / Yes, the Lord
B7
helps those that help them - selves;
F7
and the law says, what - ev - er you do's
E7
A7
G
gon - na come right back on you.
We're / We

D all mak-ing out ___ like we own ___ this ___ whole world, **G**
all move ___ a-round ___ with ob-jec - tives ___ in mind: ___

___ while the lead - ers ___ of na- **B♭**
___ to be - come ___ rich ___ or fa-

D - tions, they're act-ing like ___ big girls, ___ **F** with no thoughts ___ **A7**
- mous, with our rep - u - ta - tions signed. ___ But the few ___

D ___ for ___ their God ___ who pro - vides ___ us ___ with all. **G**
___ that ___ can reach ___ to this cov - et - ed slot ___

But when death comes to claim them, who will stand, who will fall?

don't escape old age creeping through their bodies like a rot.

Now, the Lord

Now, the Lord loves the one that loves the Lord; and the law says if you don't give, then you don't get lovin'.

Yes, / And } the Lord _____ helps _____ those _____ that help _____ them-selves; _____ and the law _____ says, what-ev-er you do's _____ gon-na come _____ right back _____ on you. _____

Now, the Lord _____

Instrumental solo

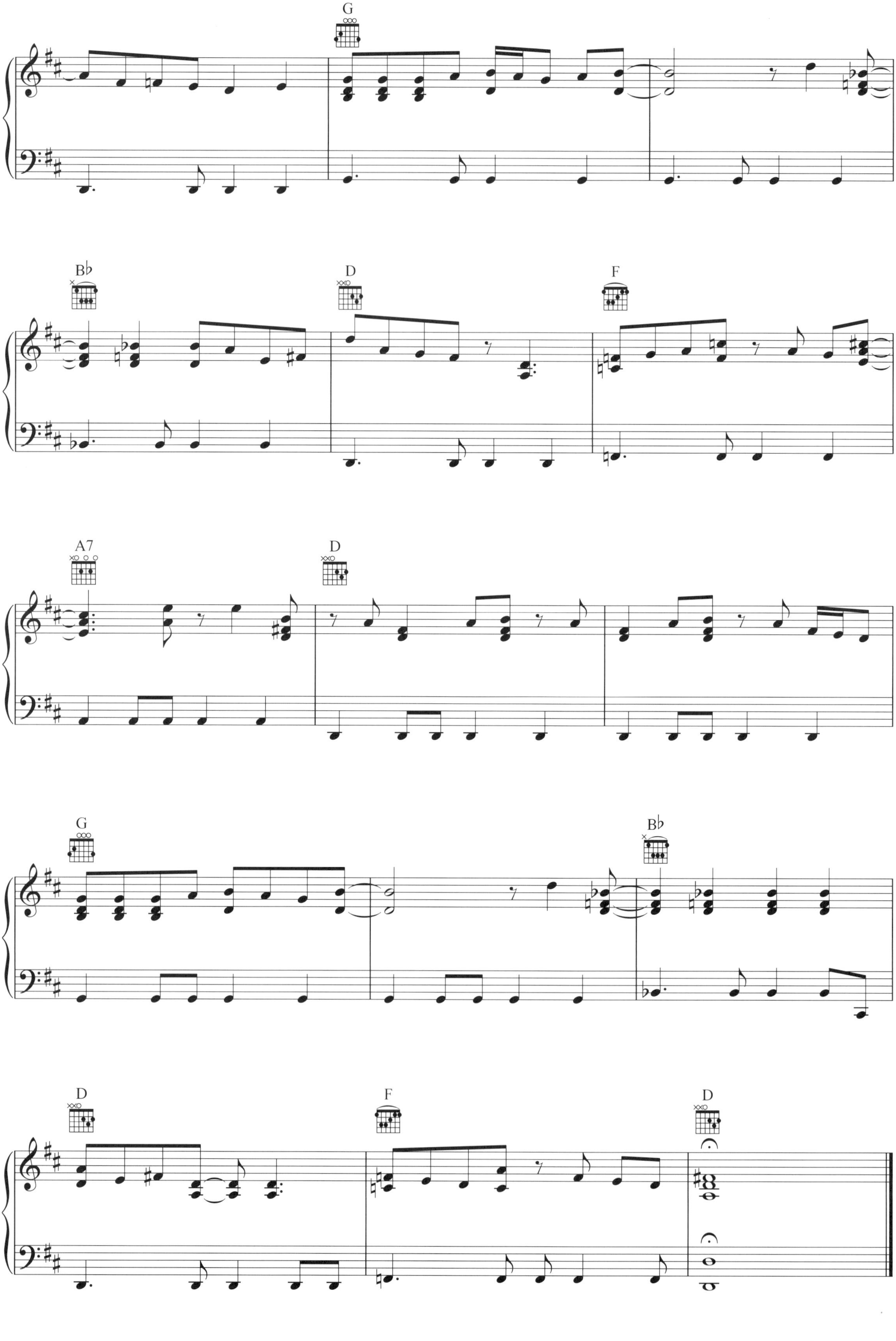
G
B♭
D
F
A7
D
G
B♭
D
F
D

MAYA LOVE

Words and Music by
GEORGE HARRISON

Moderately fast

May-a love,

May-a love,

Copyright © 1974 Umlaut Corporation
Copyright Renewed
All Rights Reserved

G
D
E7♭9
my love is like the sea
the wind
a stream
flow-ing in
blow ing hard
flow-ing in
Edim/D
D7
and out of me.
on ev - 'ry - thing.
this cos - mic dream.
3fr
To Coda
G
May - a love,
D
G♯dim7
D/A
D
May - a love,

my love is like the {day: / rain}

first it comes, then it rolls a-way.
beat-ing on your win-dow-pane.

Instrumental ad lib.

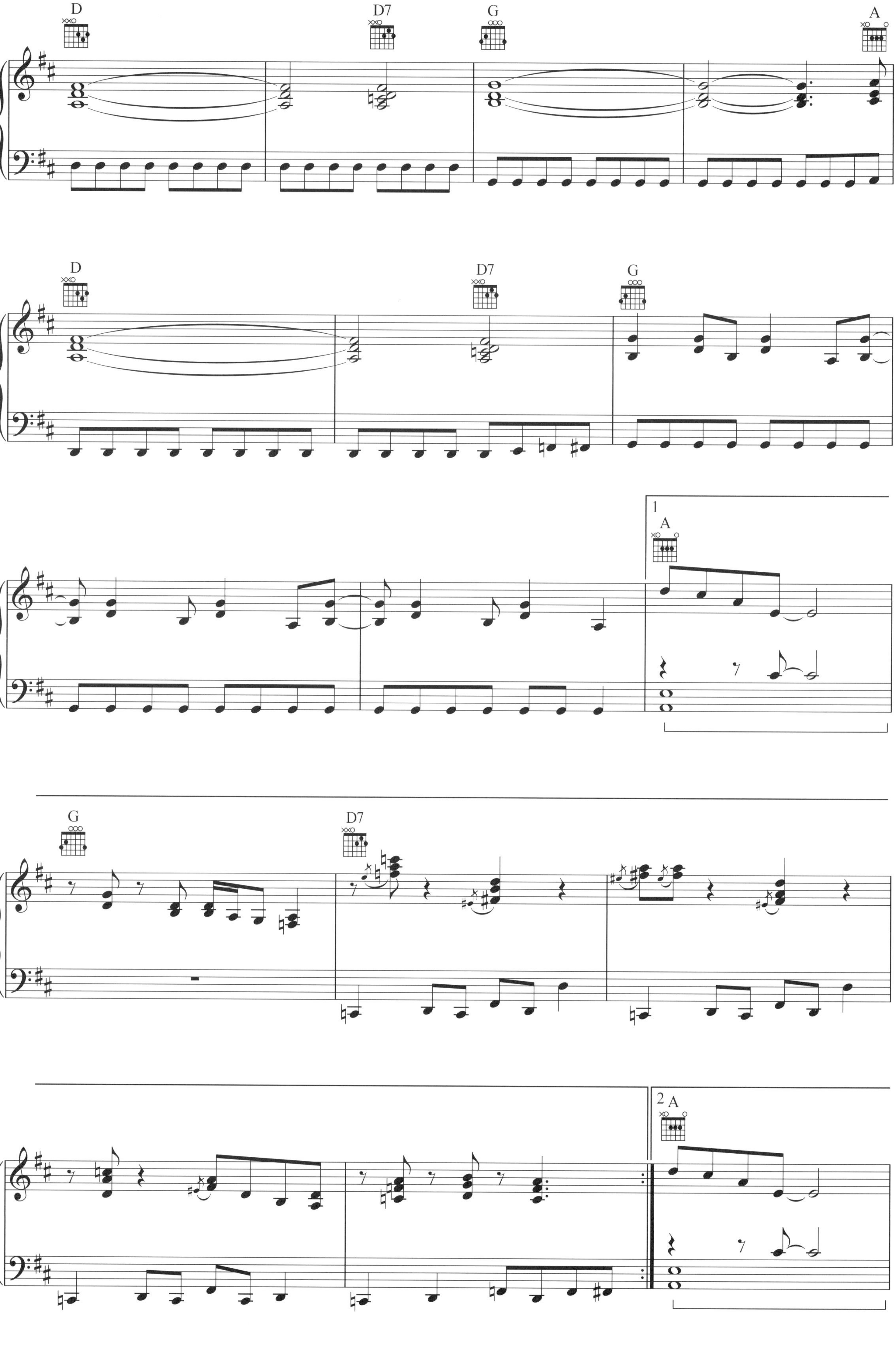
D
D7
G
A
D
D7
G
1
A
G
D7
2
A

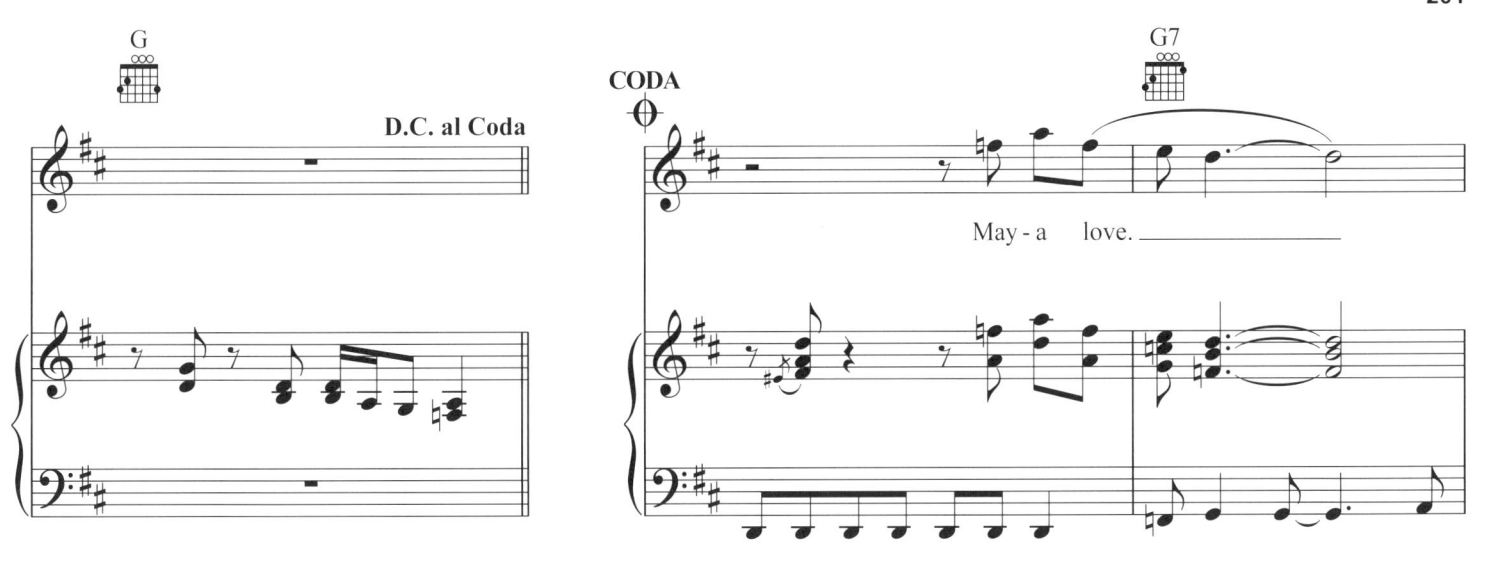

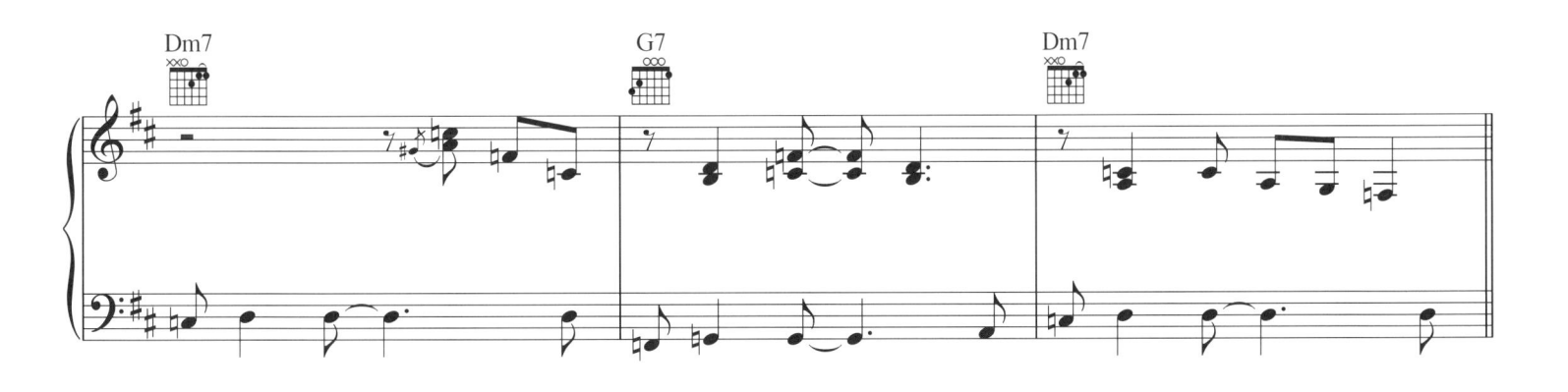

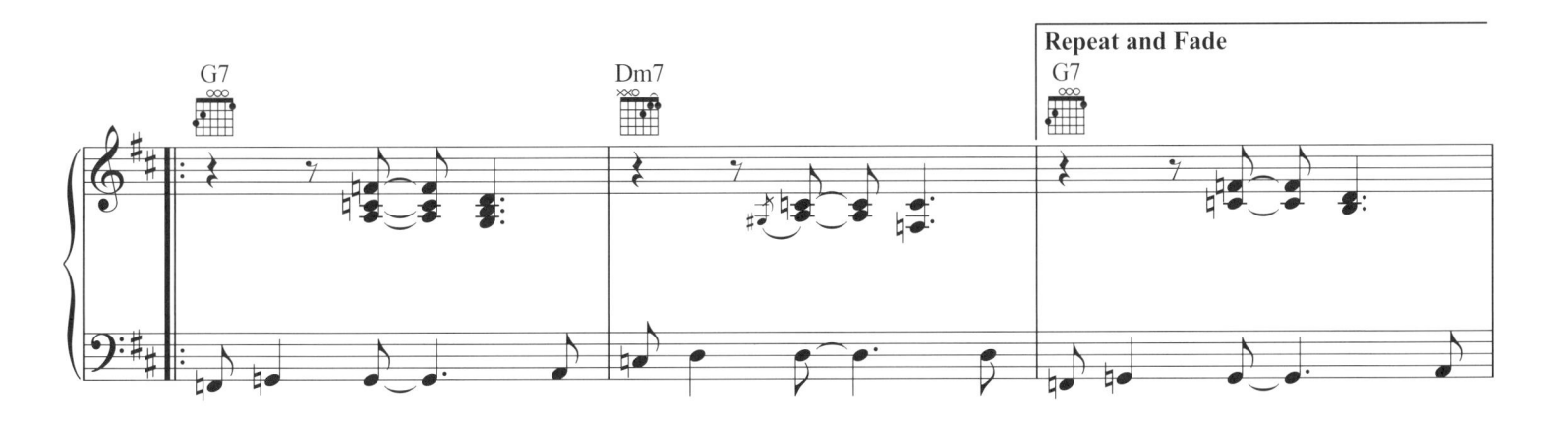

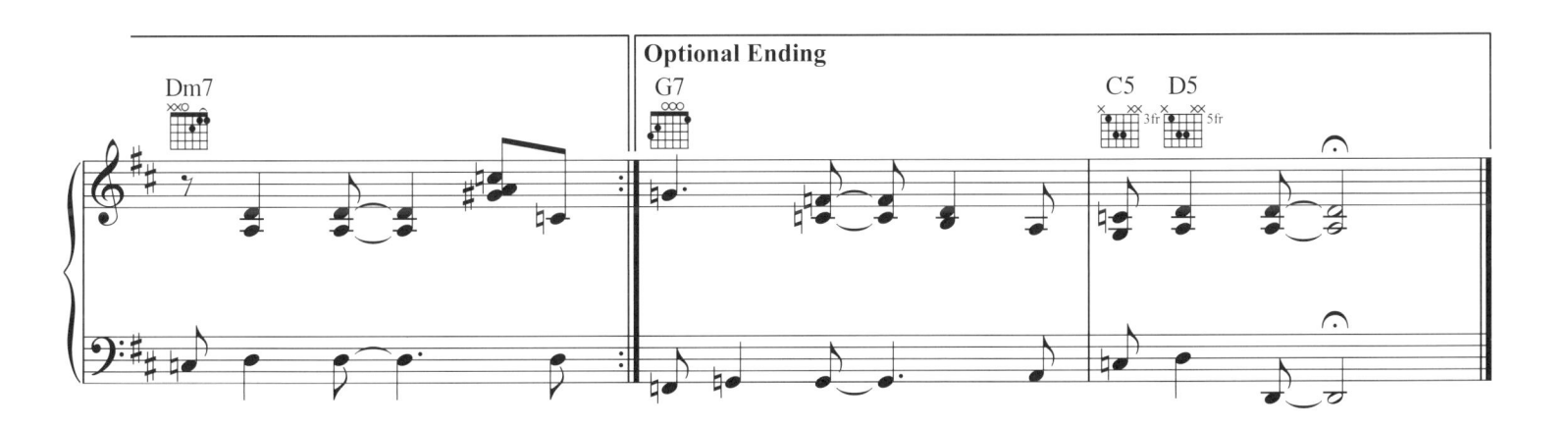

May - a love.

MISS O'DELL

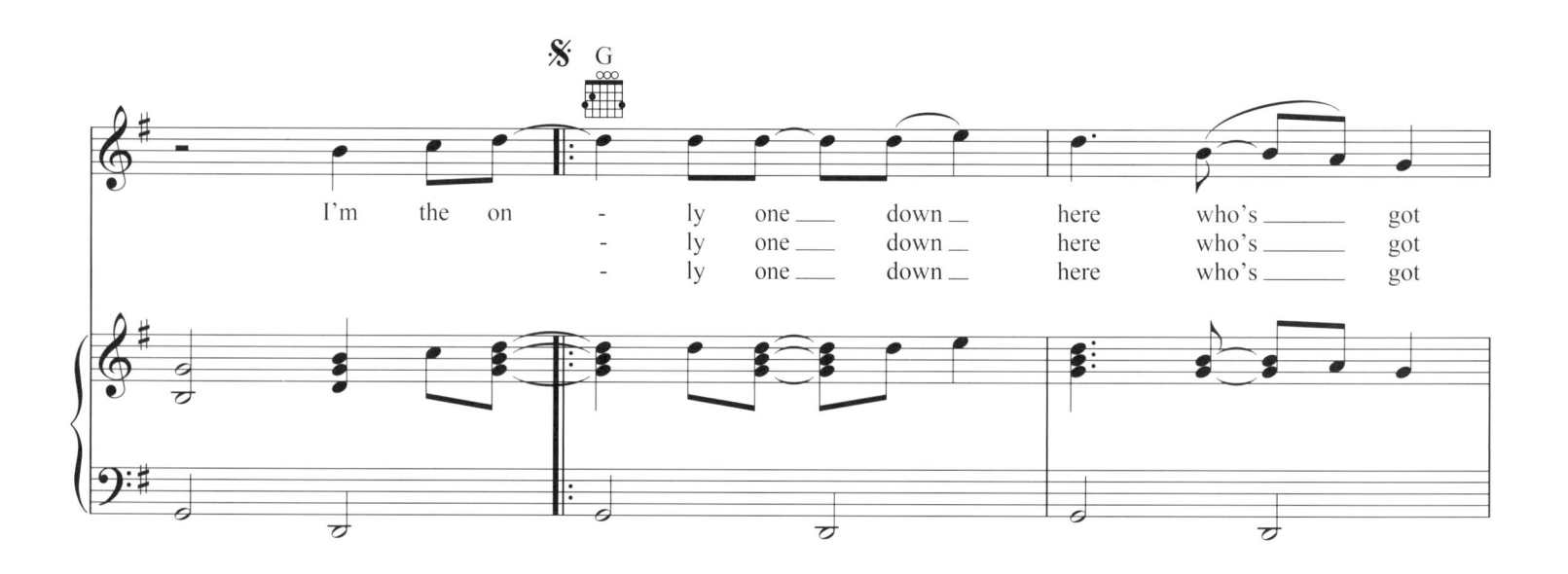

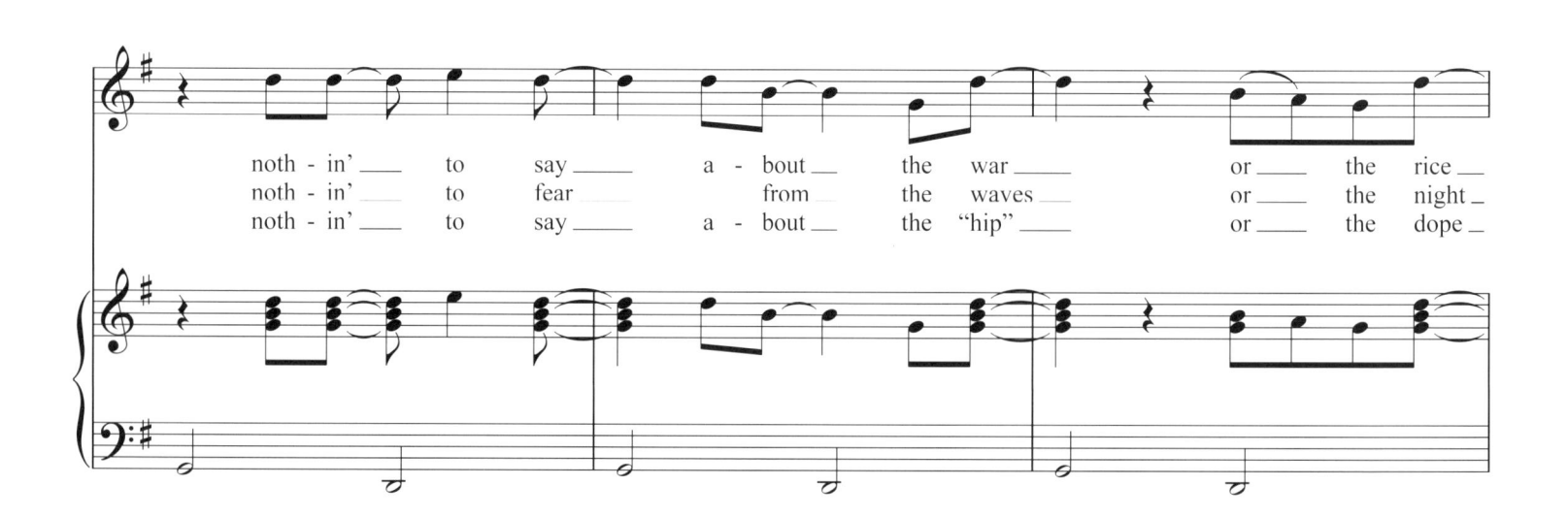

Words and Music by
GEORGE HARRISON

Moderately, in 2

I'm the on - ly one down here who's got
- ly one down here who's got
- ly one down here who's got

noth - in' to say a - bout the war or the rice
noth - in' to fear from the waves or the night
noth - in' to say a - bout the "hip" or the dope

Copyright © 1973 The Material World Charitable Foundation Ltd. and Harrisongs Ltd.
Copyright Renewed
All Rights Reserved

that keeps go - in' a - stray on its way to Bom -
that keeps roll - in' on right up to my front
or the cat with most hope to fill the Fill -

- bay.
— porch.
- more.

That smog that keeps pol - lut - ing up our
The rec - ord play - er's bro - ken on the
That push and shov - ing ring - ing on my

shores is bor - ing me to tears.
floor and Ben, he can't re - store
bell is not for me to - night.

it. Why don't you call me, Miss O'- dell?

I'm the on-

Now I can tell you

noth - ing new has

C
F
D
hap - pened since I last saw you.
D.S. al Coda
I'm the on -
CODA
C
Why don't you call me,
Bm
Miss O' - dell?
C
F
C
G

MY SWEET LORD

Words and Music by
GEORGE HARRISON

Moderately bright

Gm
C
Gm
C
mm my Lord,
mm my Lord,
F
Dm
I real - ly want to see you. Real - ly want to
I real - ly want to know you. Real - ly want to
F
Dm
F
be with you. Real - ly want to see you, Lord, but it takes
go with you. Real - ly want to show you, Lord, that it won't
F♯dim7
D7♭9
1
Gm
C
so long, my Lord. My sweet Lord,
take long— my Lord.
3fr
4fr

2
Gm C Gm
Hal - le - lu - jah. Hal - le - lu -
My sweet Lord,
C Gm C
- jah. Hal - le - lu - jah.
mm my Lord, my sweet Lord,
Gm C F
Hal - le - lu - jah.
I real - ly want to see you.
F7
Real - ly want to see you. Real - ly want to

D7
G
see you, Lord. Really want to see you, Lord, but it takes
E7♭9
Am
D
Hal - le - lu - jah.
so long, my Lord. My sweet Lord,
Am
D
Am
Hal - le - lu - jah. Hal - le - lu -
mm my Lord,
D
Am
D
- jah. Hal - le - lu - jah.
my my Lord, I real - ly want to

G
Em
G
Em
Hal - le - lu - jah.
Hal - le - lu -
know you.
Real - ly want to go with you.
- jah.
G
E7♭9
Real - ly want to show you, Lord, that it won't take long. Mm
Am
D
Am
Hal - le - lu - jah.
Hal - le - lu -
mm
D
Am
D
- jah.
Hal - le - lu - jah.
My sweet Lord,
my my Lord.

Am
D
G
Em
Hal - le - lu - jah.
G
G
G♯dim7
E7♭9
Am
D
Am
Ha - re Krish -
Mm my Lord,
D
Am
D
- na. Ha - re Krish - na.
my my my Lord, my my sweet

Am D Am
Krish - na Krish - na. Ha - re Ha -
Lord, my Lord.
D G Em
- re. Ha - re Ra - ma.
Now I real - ly want to see you. Real - ly want to
G Em G
Ha - re Ra - ma.
be with you. Real - ly want to see you, Lord, but it
G♯dim7 E7♭9 Am D
Hal - le - lu - jah.
takes so long my Lord. Ooo Lord.

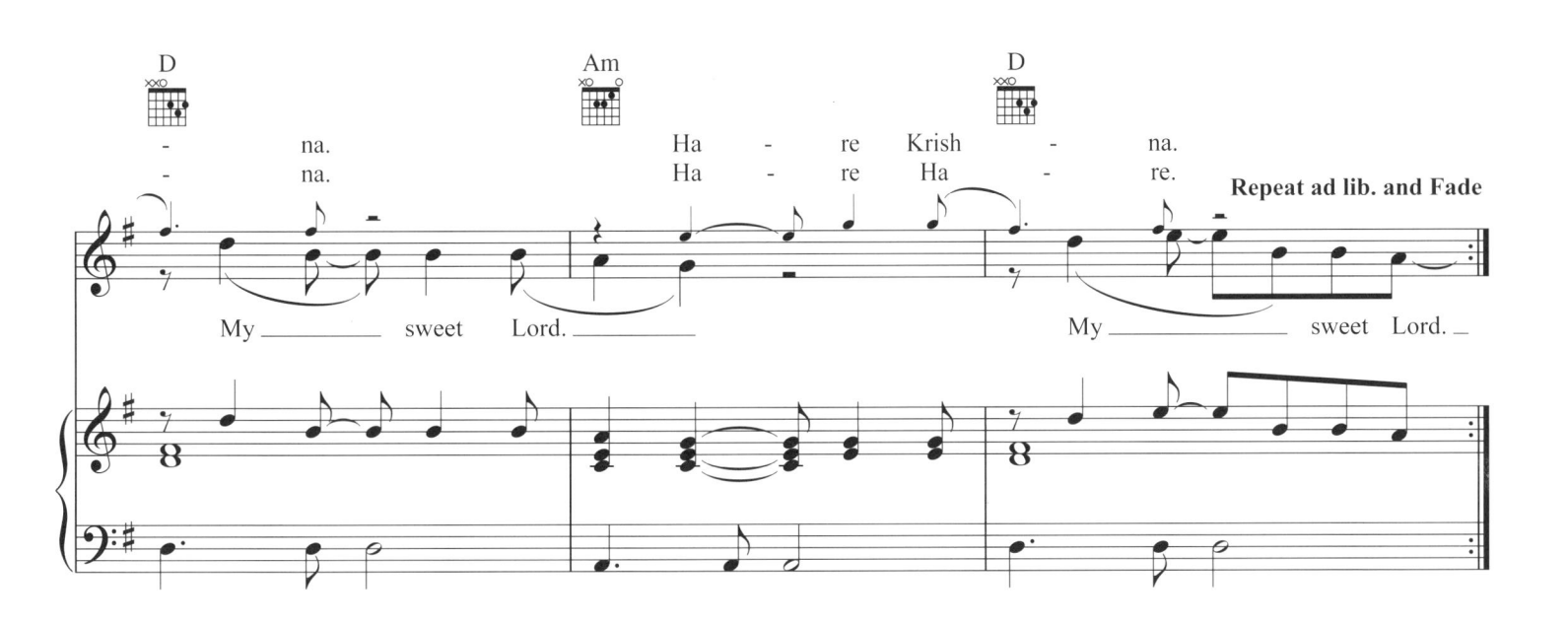

Additional Lyrics

(Gurur Brahma)
Mmmm
(Gurur Vishnu)
Mmmm
(Gurur Devo)
Mmmm
(Maheshwara)
My sweet Lord
(Gurur Sakshat)
My sweet Lord
(Parambrahma)
My my my Lord
(Tasmai Shri)
My my my my Lord
(Guruvey Namah)
My sweet Lord
(Hare Rama)
(Hare Krishna)
My sweet Lord
(Hare Krishna)
My sweet Lord
(Krishna Krishna)

OOH BABY
(You Know That I Love You)

Words and Music by
GEORGE HARRISON

Gentle Ballad

My _____ ba - by, ____ mmm ____

you know I love ____ you. ____

Copyright © 1975 Umlaut Corporation
Copyright Renewed
All Rights Reserved

D
F♯m7
My ___ ba - by, ___ ooh, ___
Gmaj7
1
F♯/A
you know I love ___ you.
Am7
I won't ___ say ___ it's for - ev - er
Cm7
A(add♯9)
A(add♭9)
5fr
3fr
right now ___ while we are to - geth - er.

2
F#/A
D
you.
F#m7
Gmaj7
1
F#/A
2
F#/A
Am7
I will be where you want
me,
Cm7
3fr
I will try to keep you hap-

-py, if on-ly you say you're my ba-by, ooh, you know I love you. My ba-by, I'd do an-y-thing for you, I'd run round the world for you, I'd do what you want me to.

Vocal ad lib. on repeat

Ooh. Know that I love you.

Repeat ad lib. and Fade

Optional Ending

RUN OF THE MILL

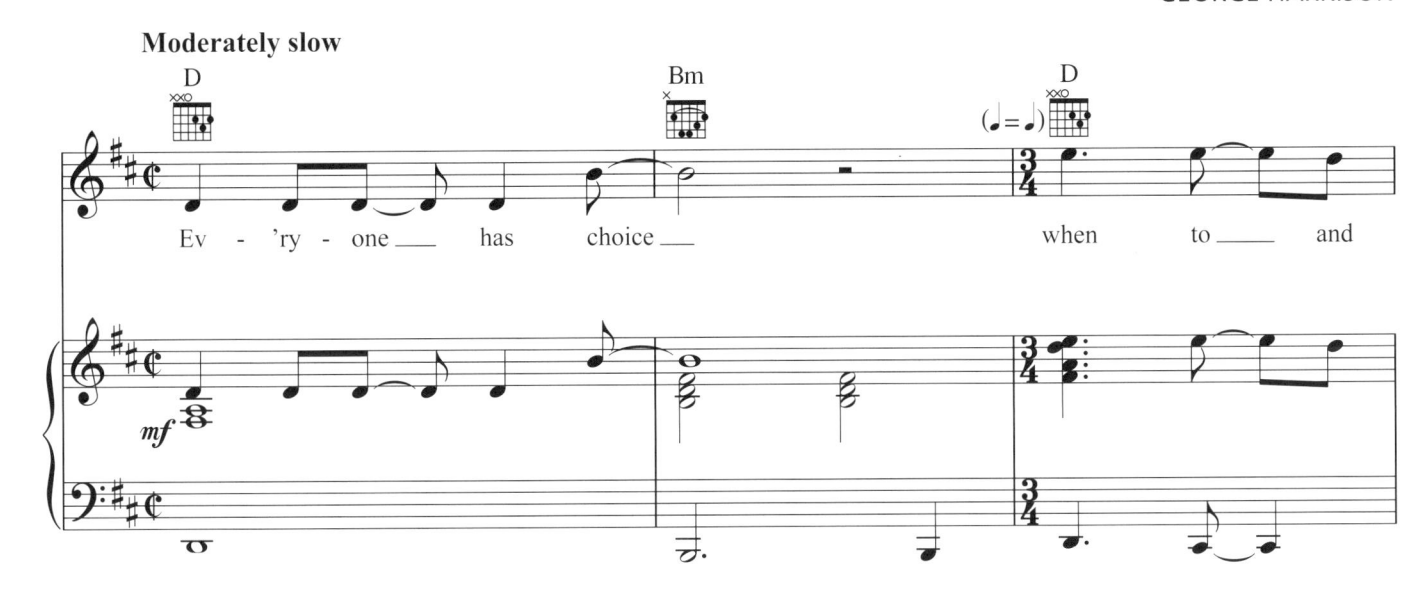

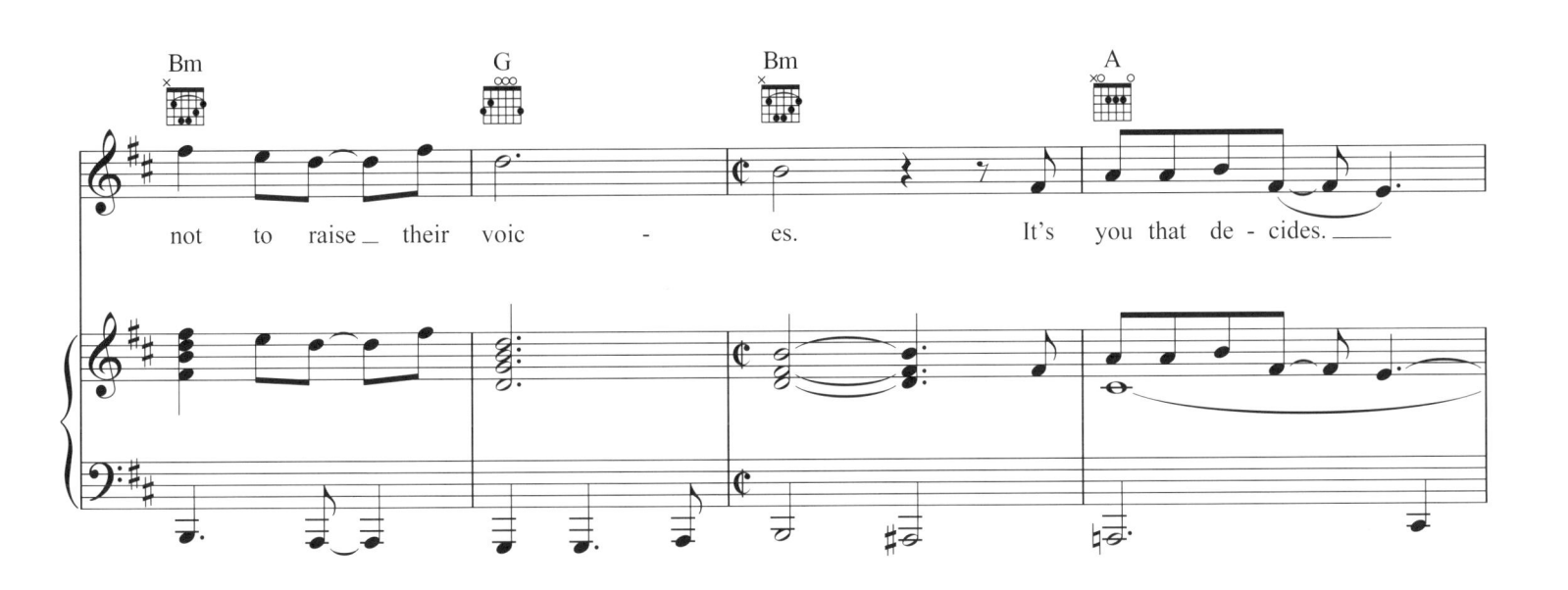

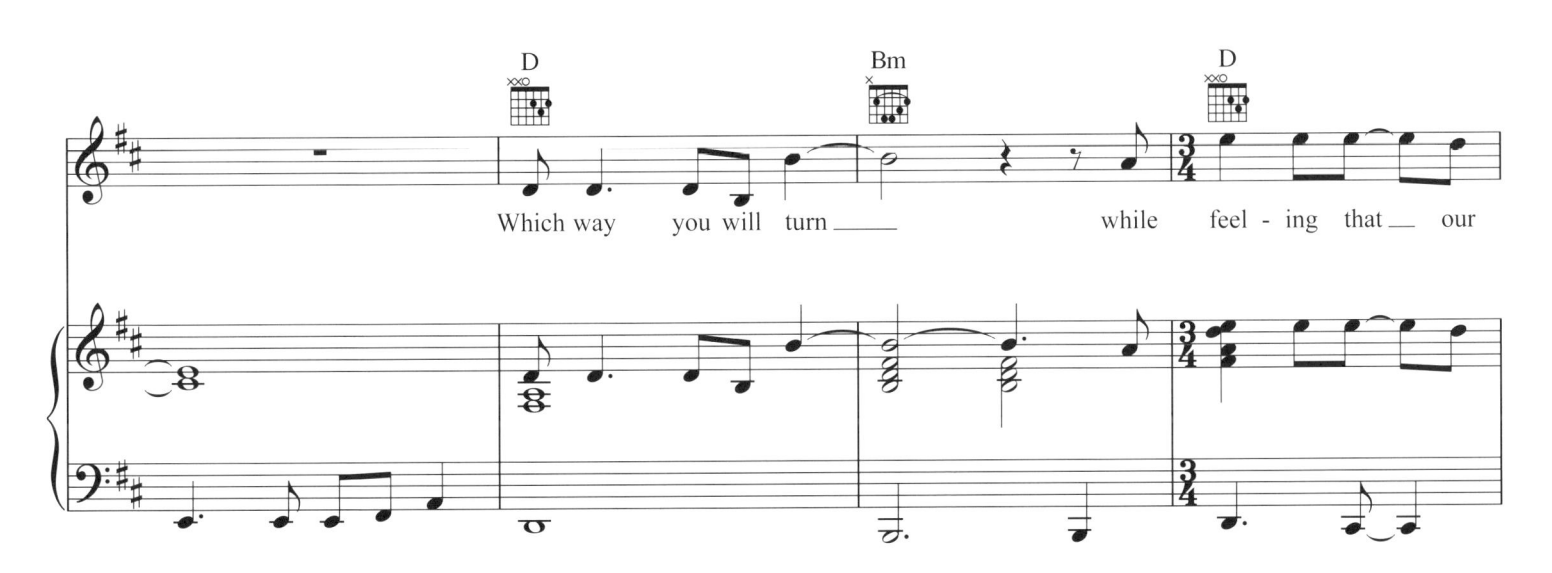

Words and Music by
GEORGE HARRISON

Moderately slow

Ev-'ry-one has choice when to and
not to raise their voic-es. It's you that de-cides.
Which way you will turn while feel-ing that our

Copyright © 1970 Harrisongs Ltd.
Copyright Renewed
All Rights Reserved

love's not your con-cern? It's you that de-cides.

No one a-round you will car-ry the blame for you. No one a-round you will love you to-day and throw it all a-way to-mor-row when you rise, an-oth - er day__ for you to re - al - ize__ me or__ send me down__ a - gain.__ As the days stand up__ on end,__ you've got me won - d'ring how I lost__ your friend - ship. But I see it in your eyes.__

Em F♯ Bm
Though I'm be - side you I can't car - ry the lame for you.
B7 Em F♯
I may de - cide to get
G F♯ D
out with your bless - ing where I'll car - ry on guess - ing how high will you leap.
Bm D Bm G
Will you make e - nough for you to reap

it? On-ly you'll ar-rive at your own made end with no one but your-self to be of-fend-ed. It's you that de-cides.

SIMPLY SHADY

Words and Music by
GEORGE HARRISON

Moderately slow

Some-body brought the juic-er; I thought I'd take a sip.
soon-er had I sown it, when I be-gan to reap.
peb-ble in the o-cean must have caused some kind of stir,

Came off the rails so cra-zy, my
I was torn from shal-low wa-ter and
and, wit-nessed by the si-lence, will

Copyright © 1974 Umlaut Corporation
Copyright Renewed
All Rights Reserved

225

is simply shady; it's all been done before, but it doesn't make life easy, that's for sure. You may think about a lady, cause yourself a minor war. Then your life won't be so easy anymore.

is simply shady; it's all been done and more, but it doesn't make life simple, that's for sure. You may think about a lady, let her in through your front door, but your life won't be so easy anymore.

is simply shady; it's all been done before, but it doesn't make life easy, that's for sure. You may think of Sexy Sadie, let her in through your front door, but your life won't be so easy anymore.

No _____ a yourself a minor war, _____ but your life _____ won't be _____ so eas - y an - y - more. _____ You may think _____ of Sex - y Sa - die, let her in _____ ...Cause _through your_ front door, but your life _won't be_ so eas - y an - y - more._

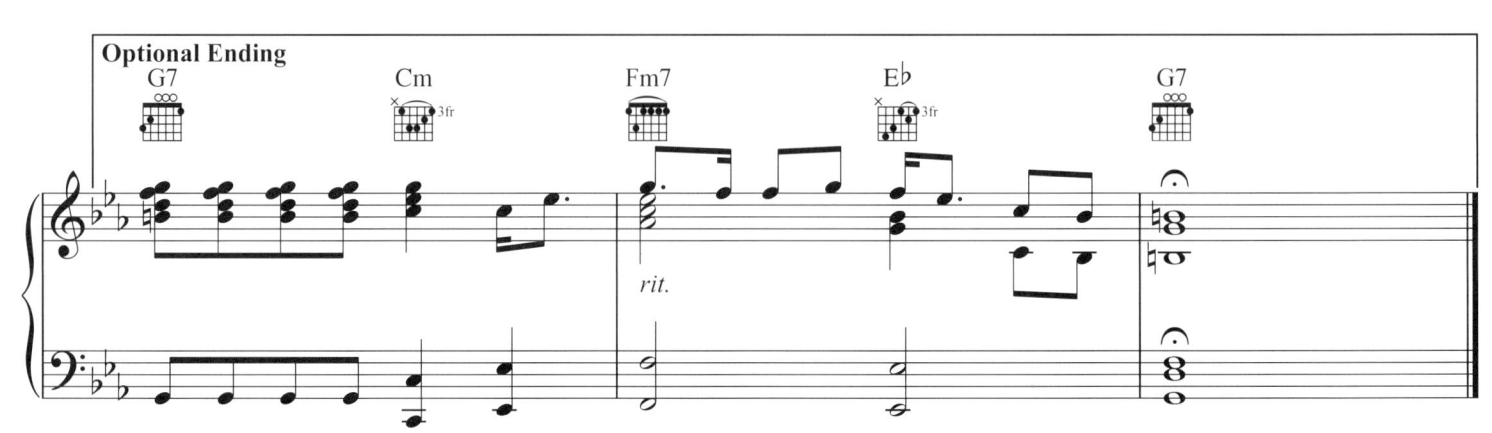

Repeat and Fade

Optional Ending

rit.

SUE ME, SUE YOU BLUES

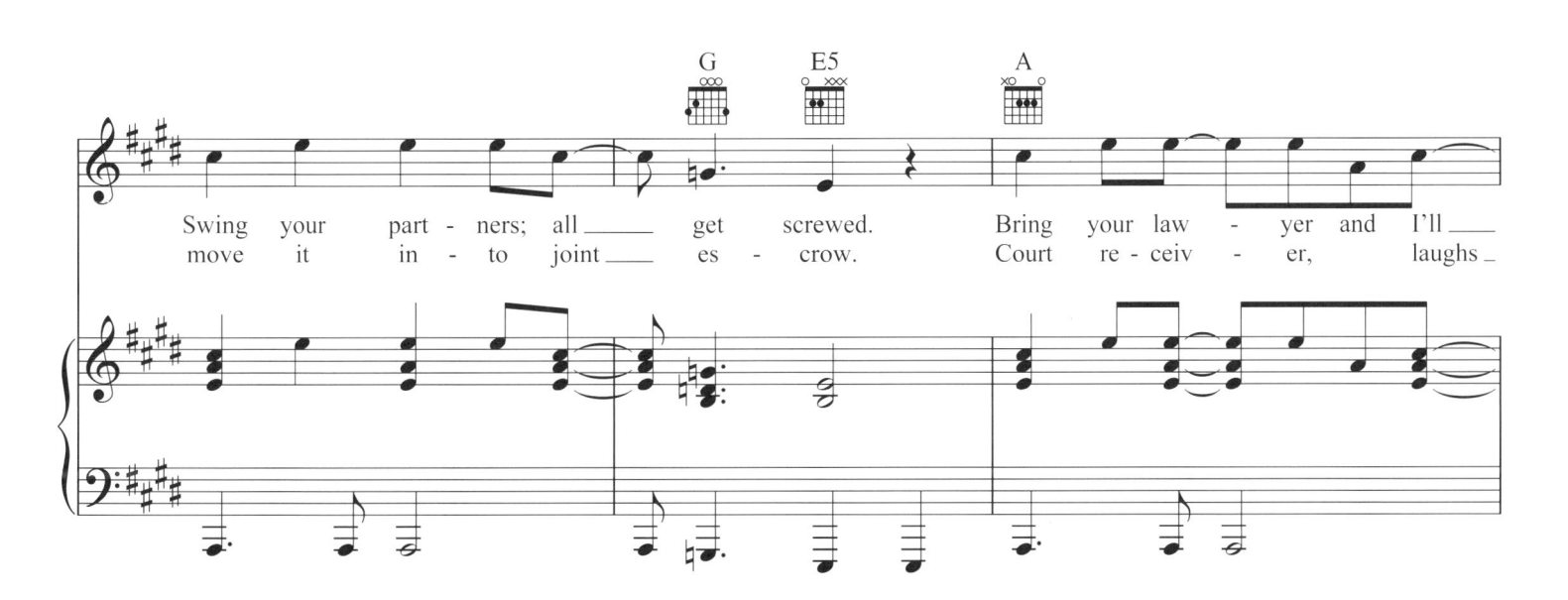

Words and Music by
GEORGE HARRISON

Moderately, in 2

1. You serve me and I'll serve you.
2. (Instrumental)
3. Hold the block on money flow. Now
4. (Instrumental)

Swing your partners; all get screwed. Bring your lawyer and I'll
move it into joint escrow. Court receiver, laughs

Copyright © 1971 Harrisongs Ltd.
Copyright Renewed
All Rights Reserved

_____ bring mine. _____ Get to-geth-er and we _____ could have _____ a bad
_____ and thrills. _____ But in the end, _____ we just pay _____ those law-yers their

time.
bills.

It's af-fi-da-vit swear-ing time. _____
When you serve me and I serve you, _____

Sign it on the dot-ted line. _____
swing your part-ners; all _____ get screwed. _____

Hold your Bi- ble in your hand. Now
Bring your law- yer and I'll bring mine.

all that's left is to find your- self a new
Get to- geth- er and we could have a bad

man.
time.

We're gon- na play the sue me, sue you

232

233

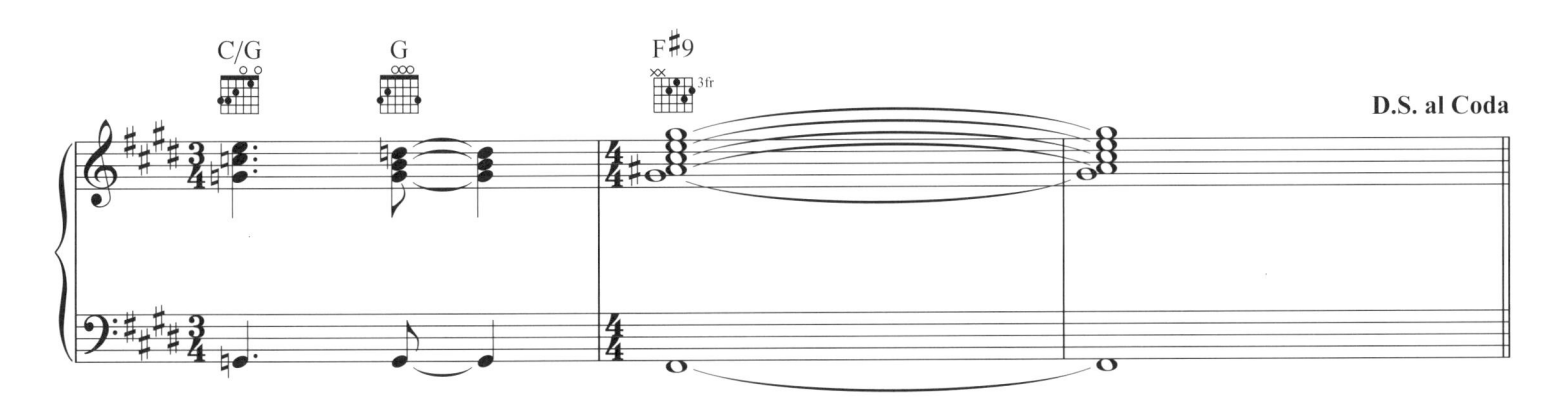

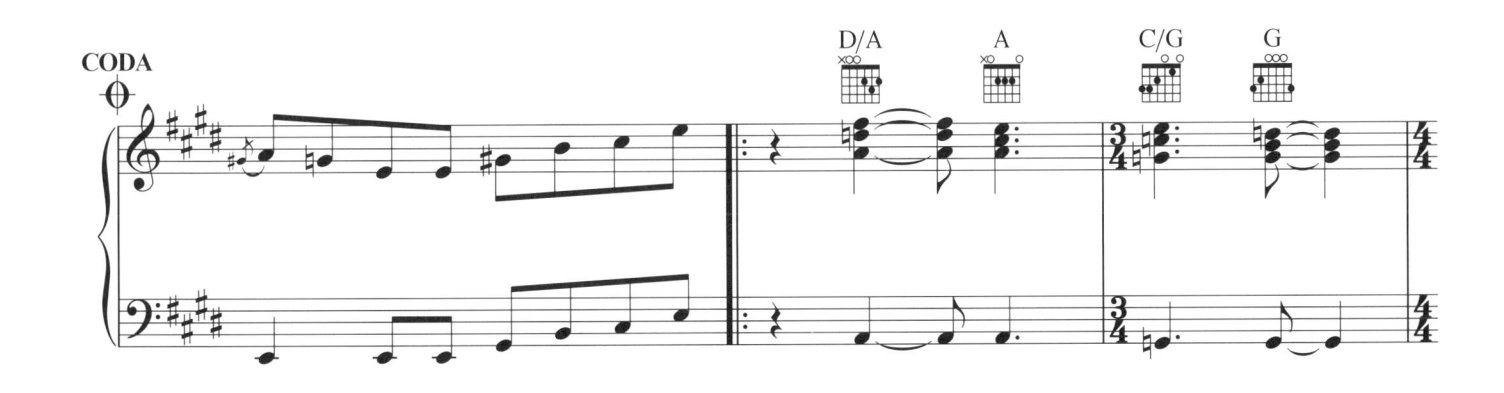

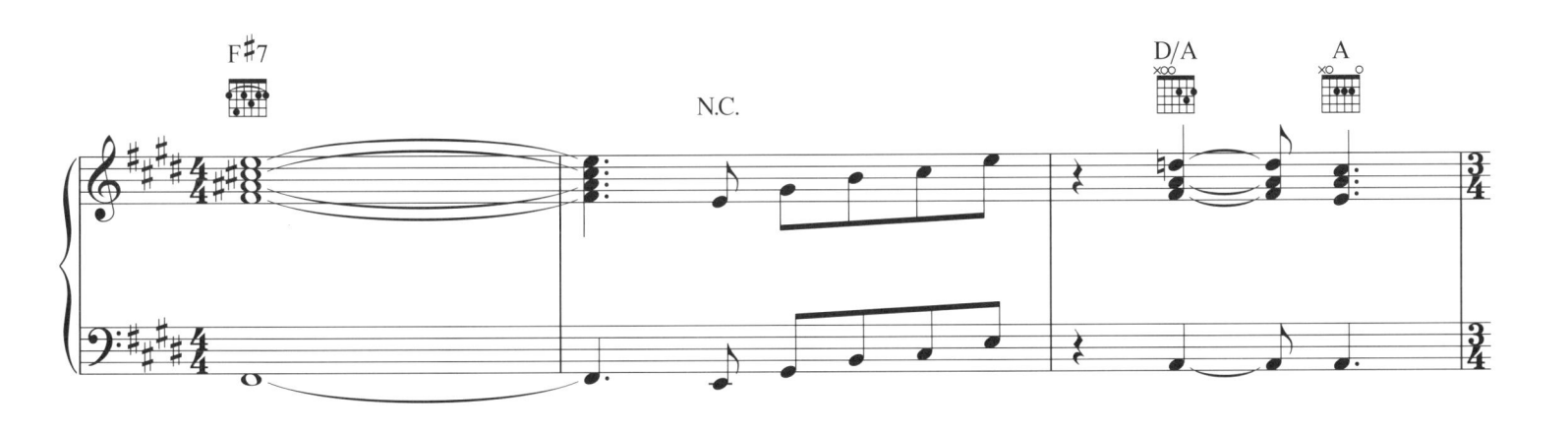

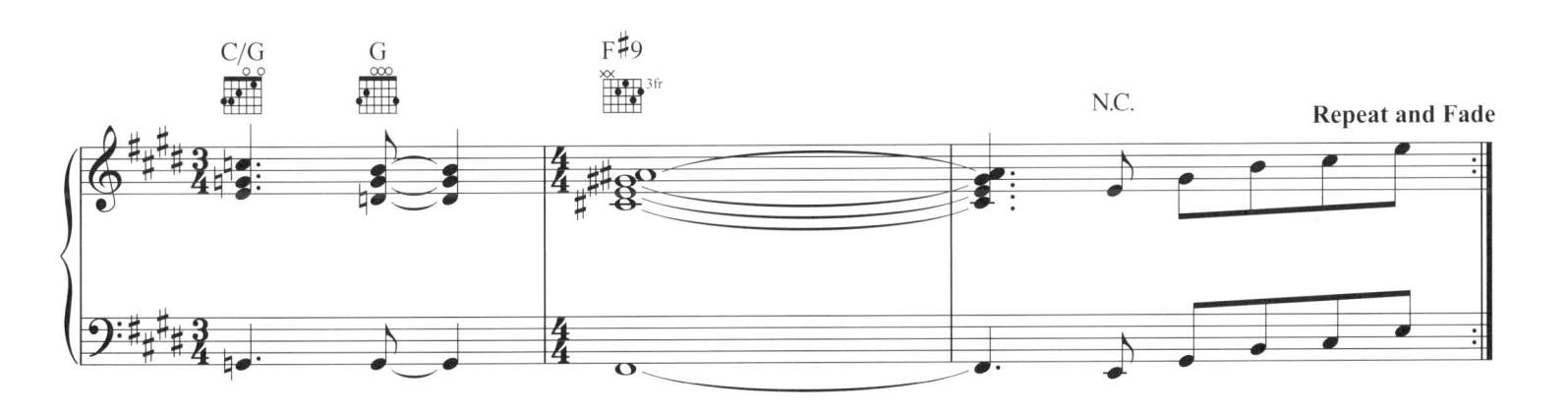

SO SAD

Words and Music by
GEORGE HARRISON

Moderately

Now the win- -ter has come,
o- -ry raced with much speed and
of the day

*Copyright © 1974 Harrisongs Ltd.
Copyright Renewed
All Rights Reserved*

-ing the sun / that has light - ed my love
and great haste / through the prob - lem of be-
it a - way / to some - one who can feel

for some time. / And a cold
-ing there, / in his heart,
a part / of the dream

wind now blows; not much ten - der-ness flows
at arm's length, held, with - in, great strength
we once held. Now it's got to be shelved.

from the heart of some - one
to ward off such a great
It's too late for to make

feeling so tired. And he feels
de-spair. But he feels
a new start. But he feels

so a-lone _with no love_ of his own._

So sad._

So bad._

So sad. _____ So bad. _____

While his mem-

So bad. _____ So sad. _____

So bad. _____

To Coda
A Em7 A7 D A Em7
So sad.
So bad.
G A7 D
D.S. al Coda
Take the dawn
CODA
A7 D A Em7 G A7 D
So bad.
So
A Em7 A D A Em7
sad.
So bad.

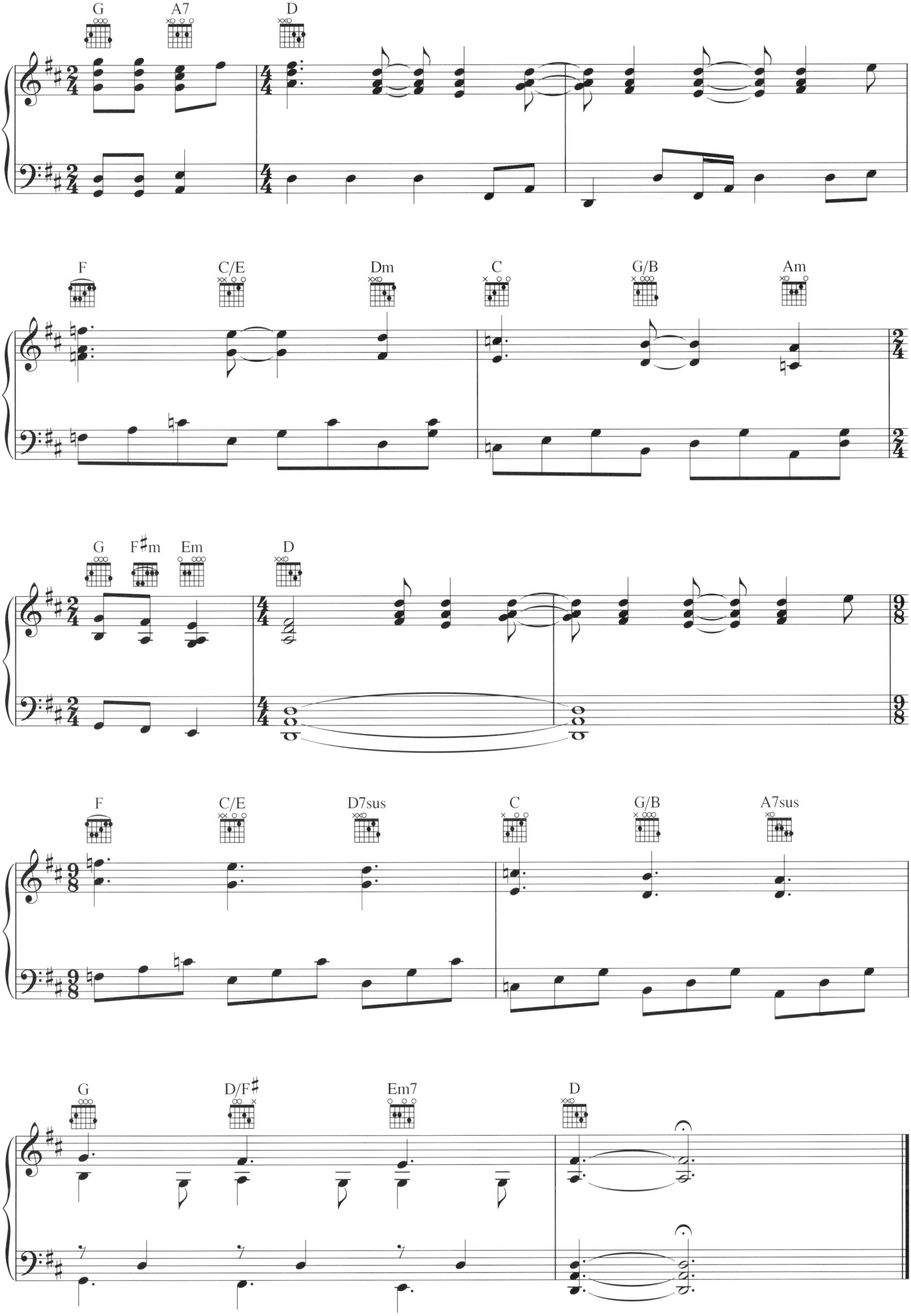
G
A7
D
F
C/E
Dm
C
G/B
Am
G
F♯m
Em
D
F
C/E
D7sus
C
G/B
A7sus
G
D/F♯
Em7
D

THAT IS ALL

Words and Music by
GEORGE HARRISON

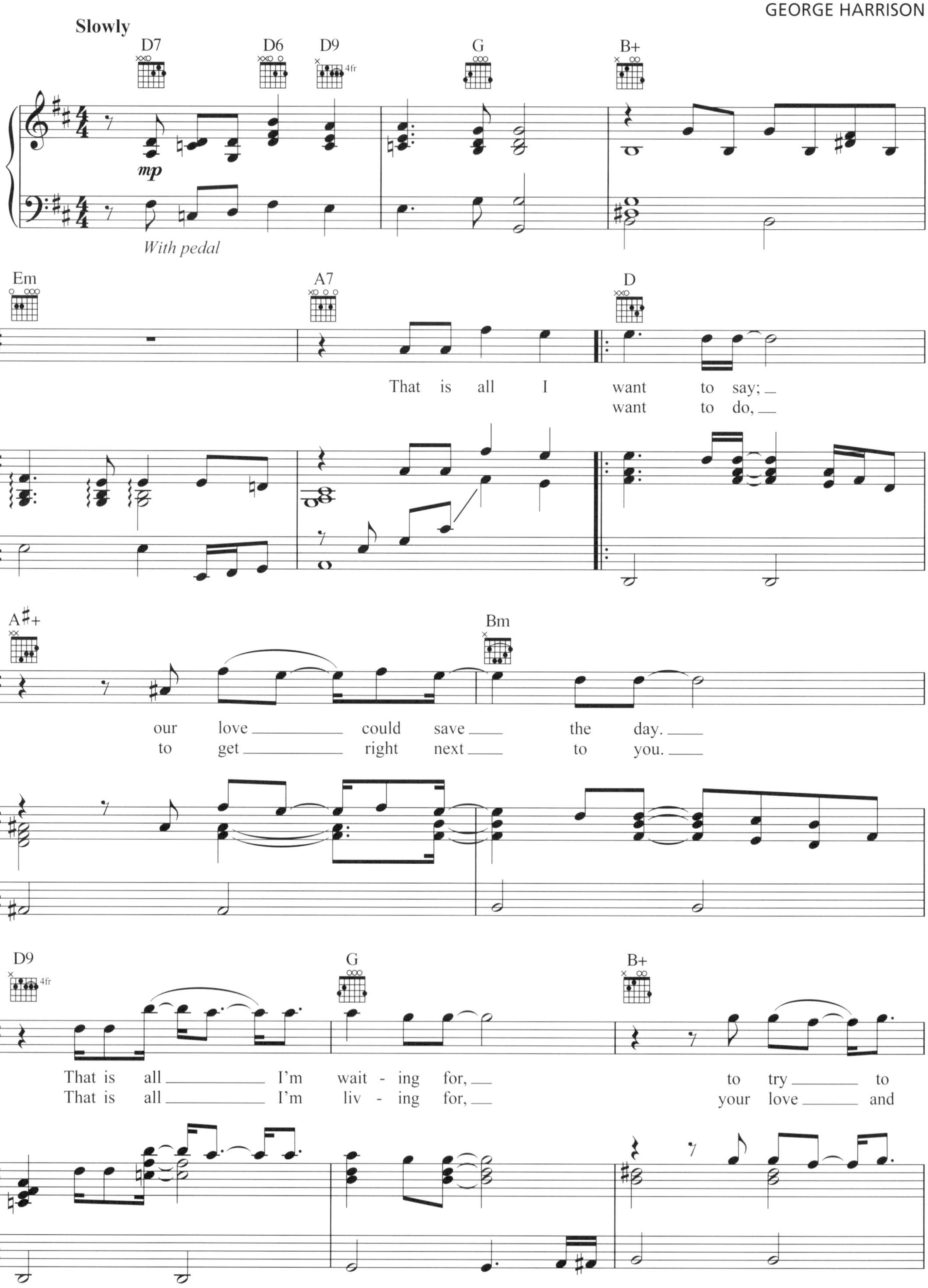

love you more. / noth-ing more,

That is all I and that is all.

Times I find it hard to say with

use-less words get-ting in my way.

Si - lence of-ten says much more than

tryn' to say ____ what's _ been said ____ be - fore. ____

That is all ____ I want from you, ____
But that is all ____ I want to do, ____

a smile ____ when I ____ feel blue. ____
to give ____ my love ____ to you. ____

And that is all _____ I'm wait - ing for, ____
That is all _____ I'm liv - ing for; ____

your love _____ and noth - ing more, ___
please let _____ me love you more, ___

and that is all. _____

and that is all. _____

THIS GUITAR
(Can't Keep from Crying)

Words and Music by
GEORGE HARRISON

Found my-self out on a limb, but I'm hap-pi-er than I have ev-er been. But

Copyright © 1975 Umlaut Corporation
Copyright Renewed
All Rights Reserved

this guitar ____ can't keep ____ from cry-ing. ____

Learned to get up when I fall, can e-ven climb ____ the Roll-ing Stone walls. ____ This gui-tar can't keep ____ from cry-ing. This

here gui-tar can feel quite sad, can be high strung, some-times get mad. Can't un-der-stand or deal with hate, re-sponds much bet-ter to love. Thought by now you knew the score, you missed the point just like before.

This gui-tar can't keep from cry - ing.

This gui-tar, it can't keep

D7
Gm
1
D7
from cry - ing.
2
B♭
F
This here gui - tar can feel quite sad,
F/E♭
D7
Gm
can be high strung, some - times get mad.
Cm
B♭
It can't un - der - stand or deal with hate, re - sponds

much bet-ter to love.

While you at-tack, cre-ate of-fence,

I'll put it down to your ig-no-rance. But this gui-tar, it can't

keep from cry-ing.

This guitar can't keep from crying.

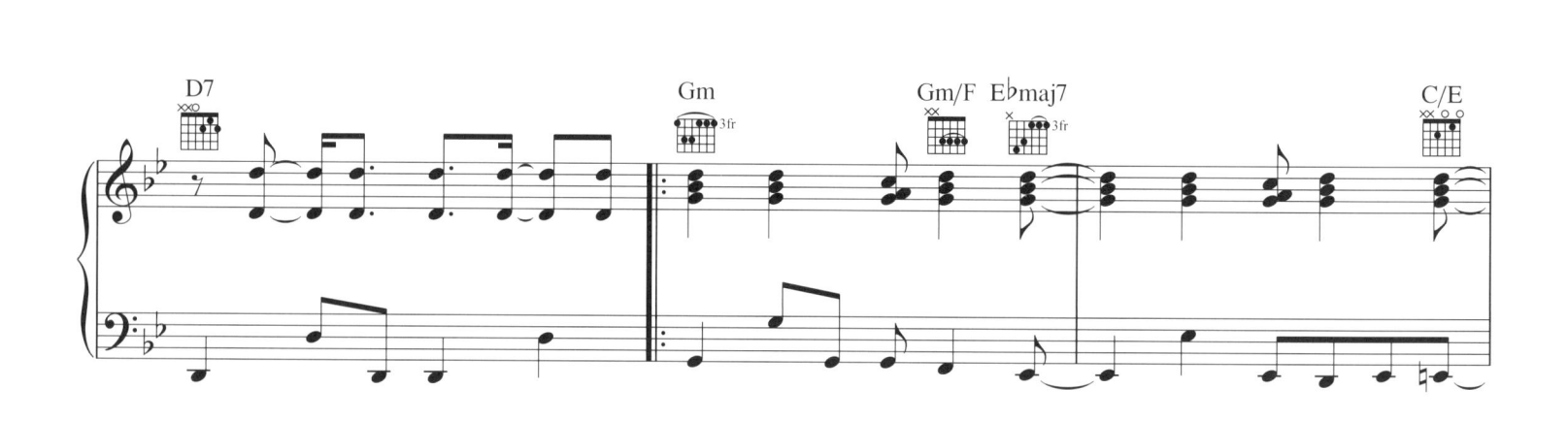

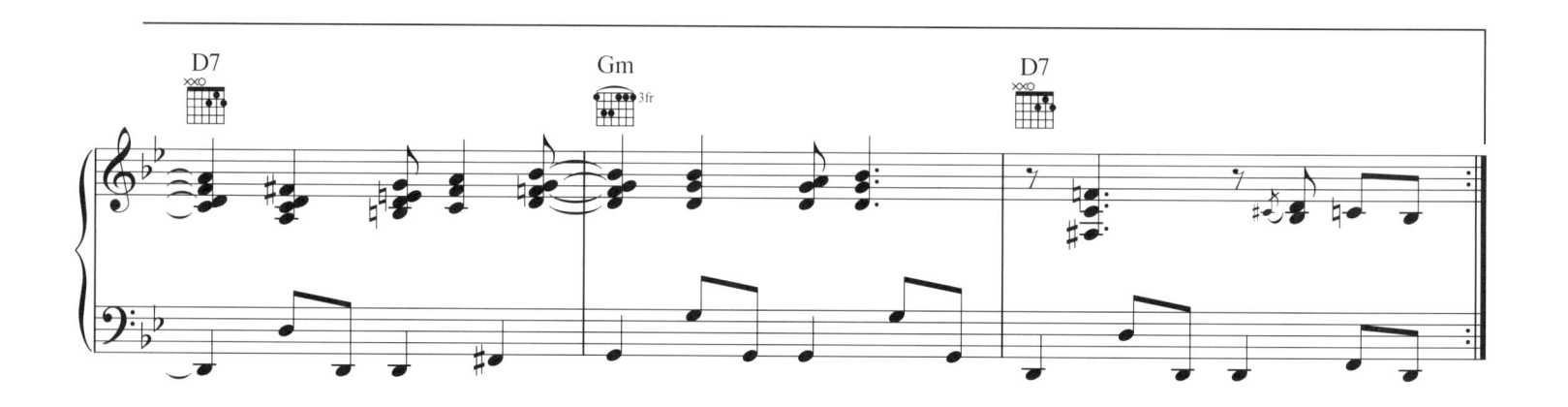

2
B♭
D7
Gm
This gui - tar can't keep from cry - ing.
D7
Gm
Gm/F
E♭maj7
C/E
E♭/G
E♭/F
B♭
This gui - tar can't keep
Vocal tacet on repeat
from cry - ing.
D7
Gm
D7
Repeat and Fade
Optional Ending
Gm

TIRED OF MIDNIGHT BLUE

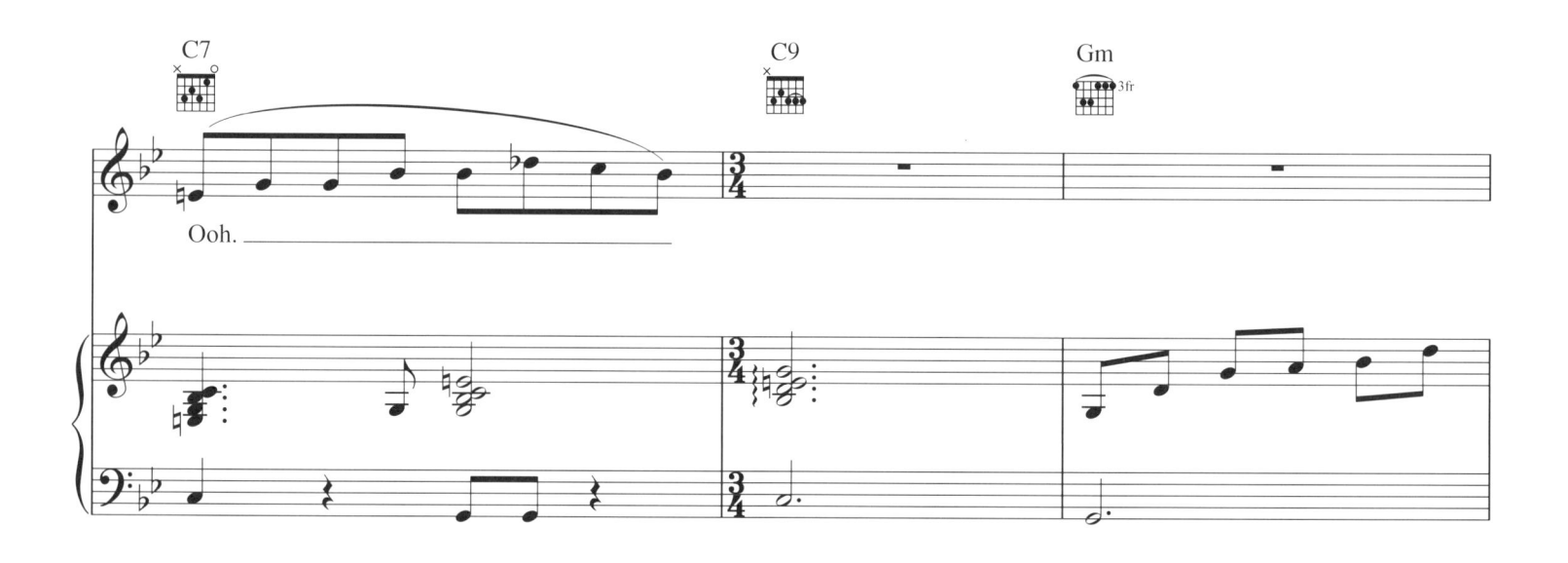

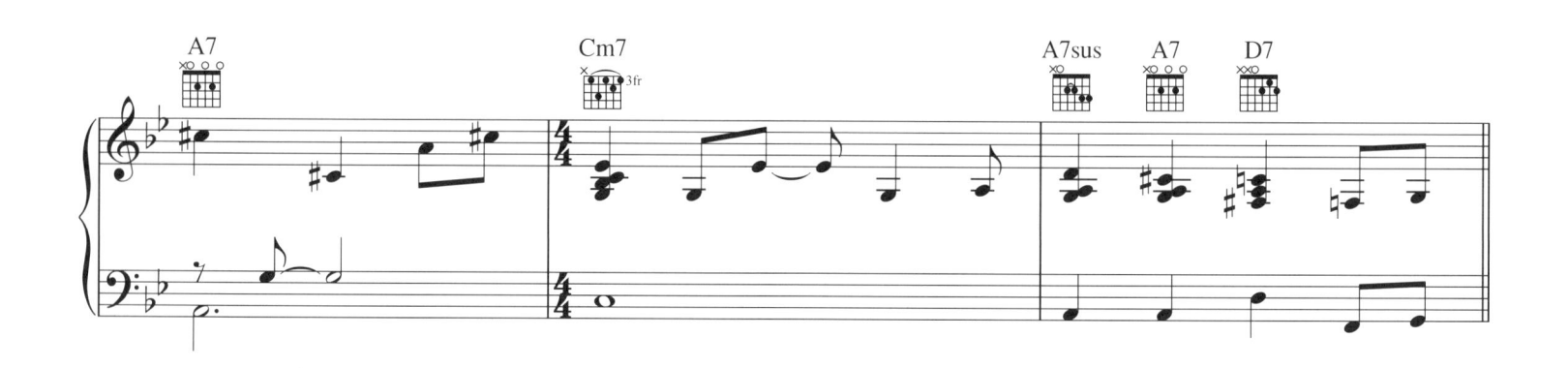

Words and Music by
GEORGE HARRISON

With a groove

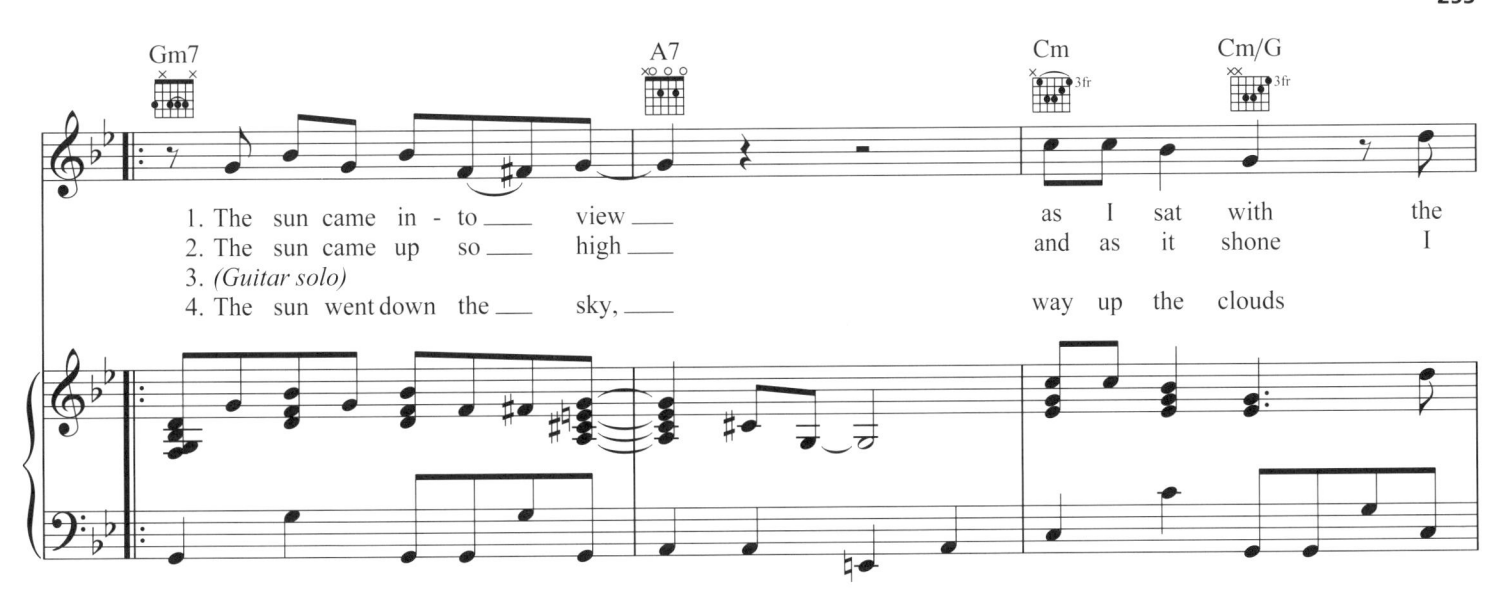

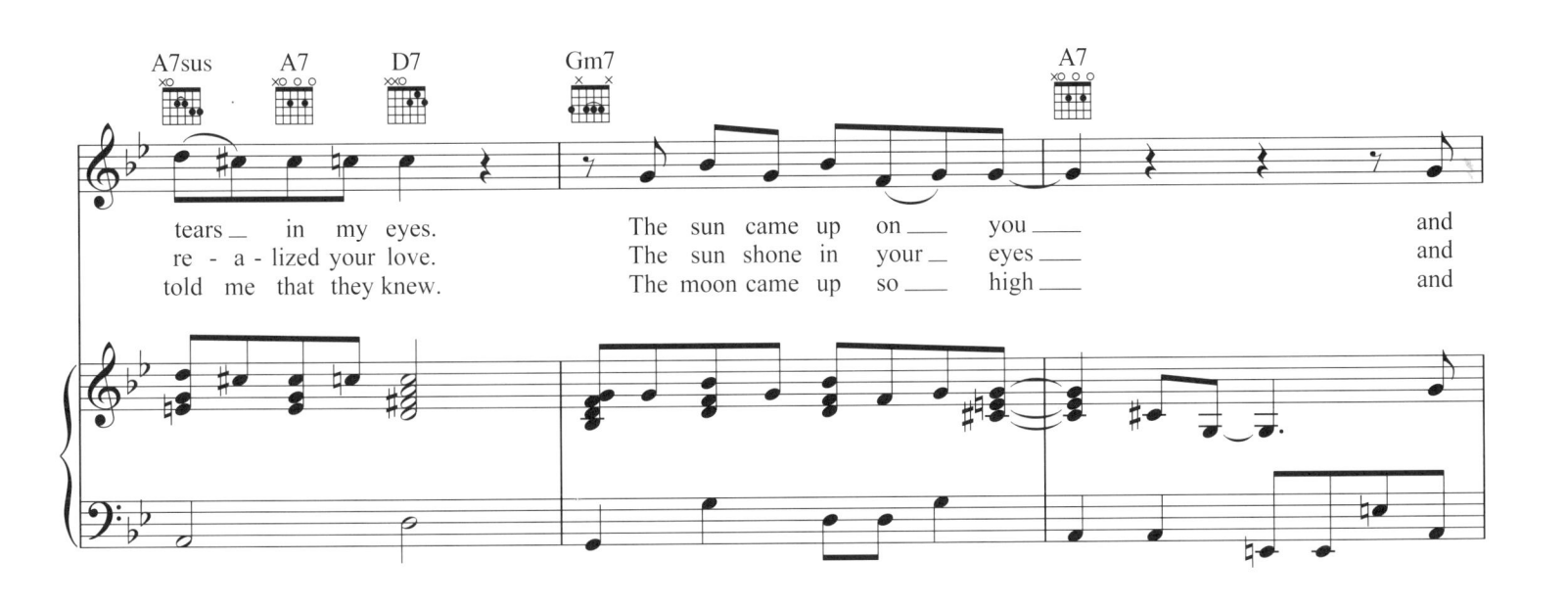

1. The sun came in-to view as I sat with the
2. The sun came up so high and as it shone I
3. *(Guitar solo)*
4. The sun went down the sky, way up the clouds

tears in my eyes. The sun came up on you and
re-a-lized your love. The sun shone in your eyes and
told me that they knew. The moon came up so high and

as you smiled, the tear-drop, it dried.
as you smiled, you re-a-lized it too.
as you smiled, I knew that you knew too.

Don't know where I had been,

but I know what I _____ have seen. _____

Made me chill right to the bone, _____

made me wish that I'd _____ stayed home _____ a - lone with you.

Tired of mid-night blues. _____

Oh.

Oh.

I don't know where I had been, but I know what I have seen.

Made me chill right to the bone, _____ made _____ me wish _____ that I'd _____ stayed _____ home _____ with you.

Oh. _____ Oh. _____

C7
D+
D7
Oh.
Oh.
D7sus
D7
C7
Csus2
3fr
Oh.
Gm
3fr
A7
Cm
3fr
Gm
3fr
Oh.
A7
Repeat and Fade
Cm
3fr
Optional Ending
Cm
3fr
Gm
3fr
rit.

TRY SOME BUY SOME

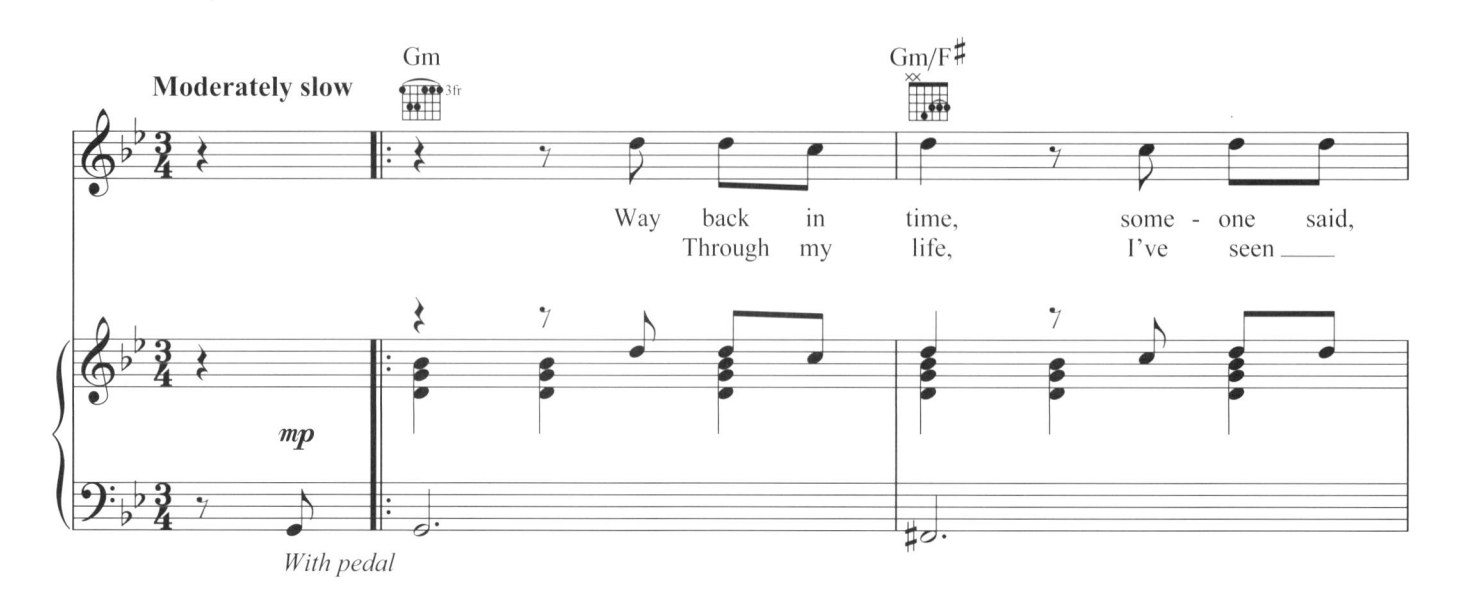

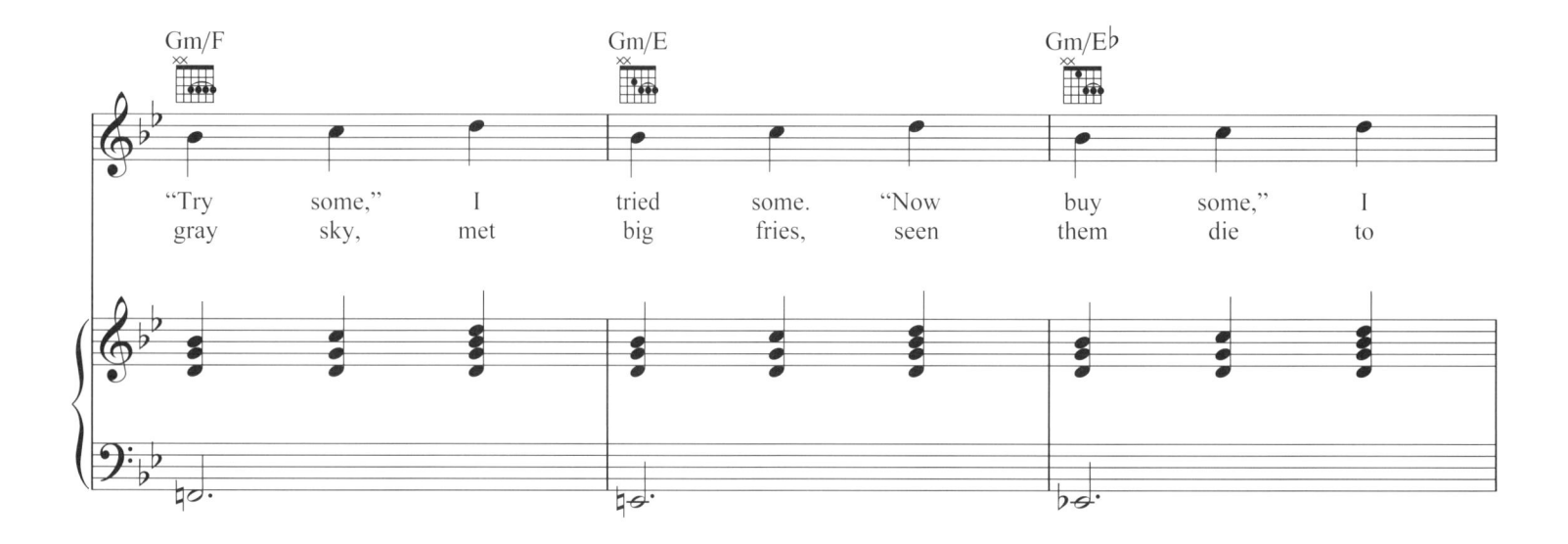

Words and Music by
GEORGE HARRISON

Moderately slow

Way back in time, some-one said,
Through my life, I've seen

"Try some," I tried some. "Now buy some," I
gray sky, I met big fries, seen them die to

bought some. Oh, whoa whoa. After a
get high. And when it

Copyright © 1971 Harrisongs Ltd.
Copyright Renewed
All Rights Reserved

| Cm/B | Cm/B♭ | Cm/A |

while, when I had tried them, de - nied them, I
seemed that I would al - ways be lone - ly, I

| Cm/A♭ | Cm/G | F#dim7 |

o - pened my eyes and I saw you.
o - pened my eyes and I saw you.

| F7 | B♭ |

Not a thing
Not a thing

did I have, not a
did I feel, not a

thing did I see, till I
thing did I know, till I

called on your love
called on your love;

and your love came to me.
and your love sure did grow.

Whoa, _____ whoa, _____ whoa.

Whoa, _____ oh, _____ whoa.

E♭/B♭
B♭
1
2
B♭
B♭/A♭
B♭+/F♯
E♭m
E♭m/G♭
G♭7/F♭
G♭7/D♭
G♭7/F♭
G♭7/D♭
G♭7/B♭
G♭7/D♭
G♭7/B♭
G♭7
G♭7/A♭
G♭7/B♭
G♭7/C♭
G♭7/D♭
G♭7/E♭
G♭7/F♭
G♭7
D♭m/A♭
B♭
B♭/A

B♭/G
B♭/F
Edim7
E♭/B♭
B♭
B♭maj7/F
Won't you try some?
B♭
B♭maj7/F
B♭
B♭maj7/F
Yeah, won't you buy some?"
B♭
Repeat and Fade
B♭maj7/F
"Won't you
Optional Ending
B♭maj7/F
B♭
6fr

WAH-WAH

Words and Music by
GEORGE HARRISON

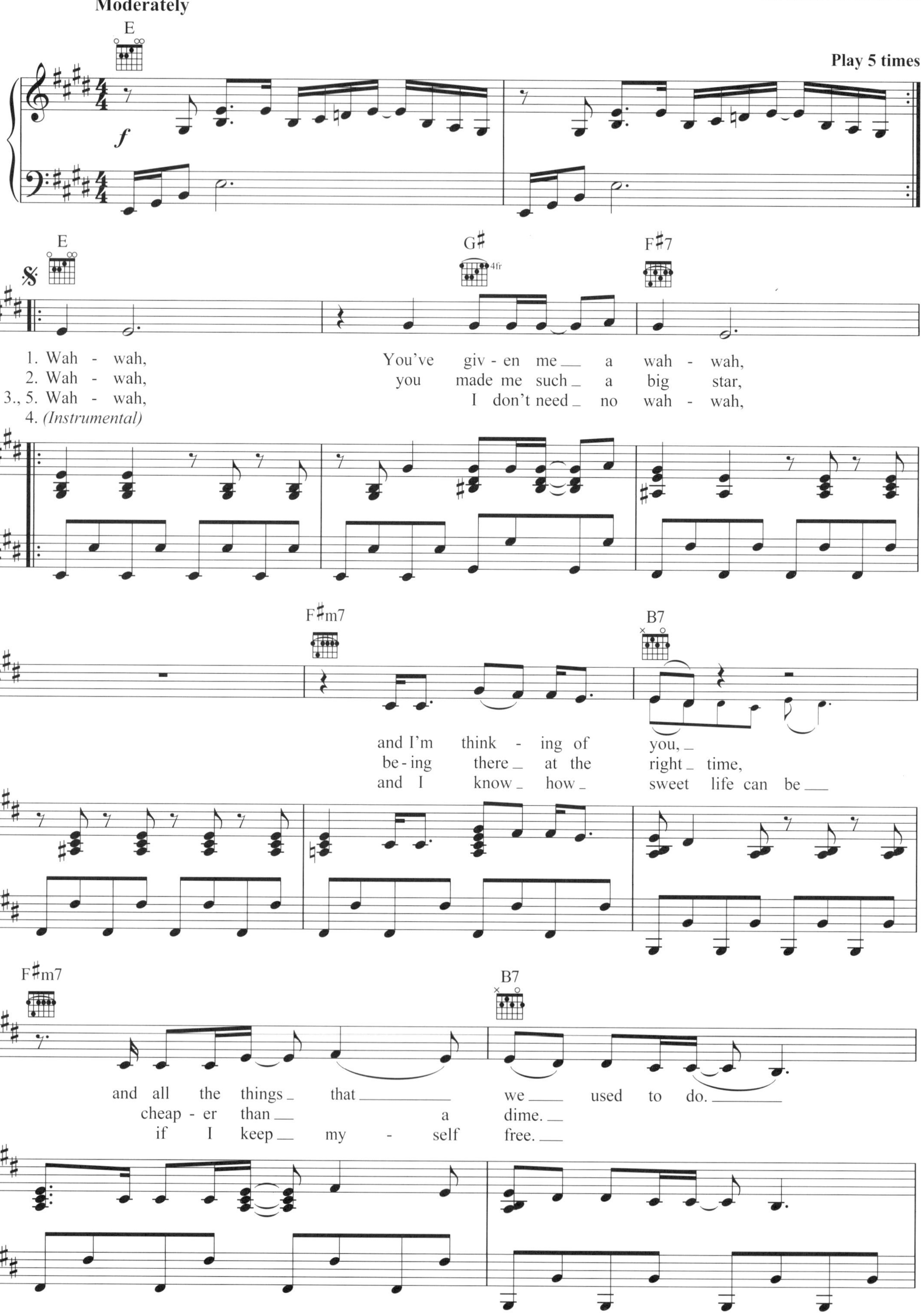

Wah - wah, you've giv-en me a wah - wah.
Wah - wah, wah - wah.
Wah - wah, I don't need no wah - wah.

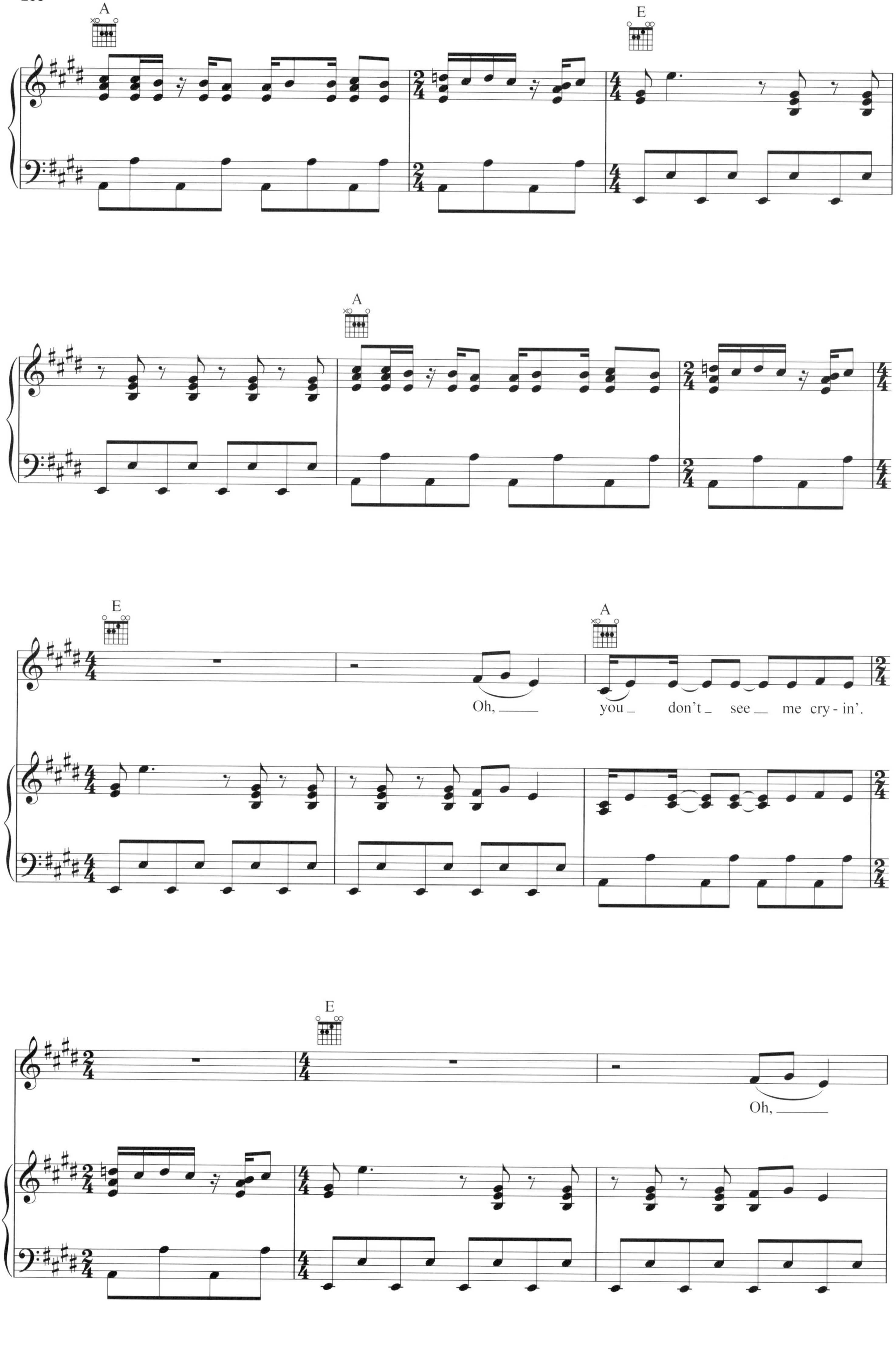
A
E
A
E
A
Oh, you don't see me cry-in'.
E
Oh,

you don't see me sigh-in'.

Wah - wah,

Repeat and Fade

wah - wah.

WHAT IS LIFE

Words and Music by
GEORGE HARRISON

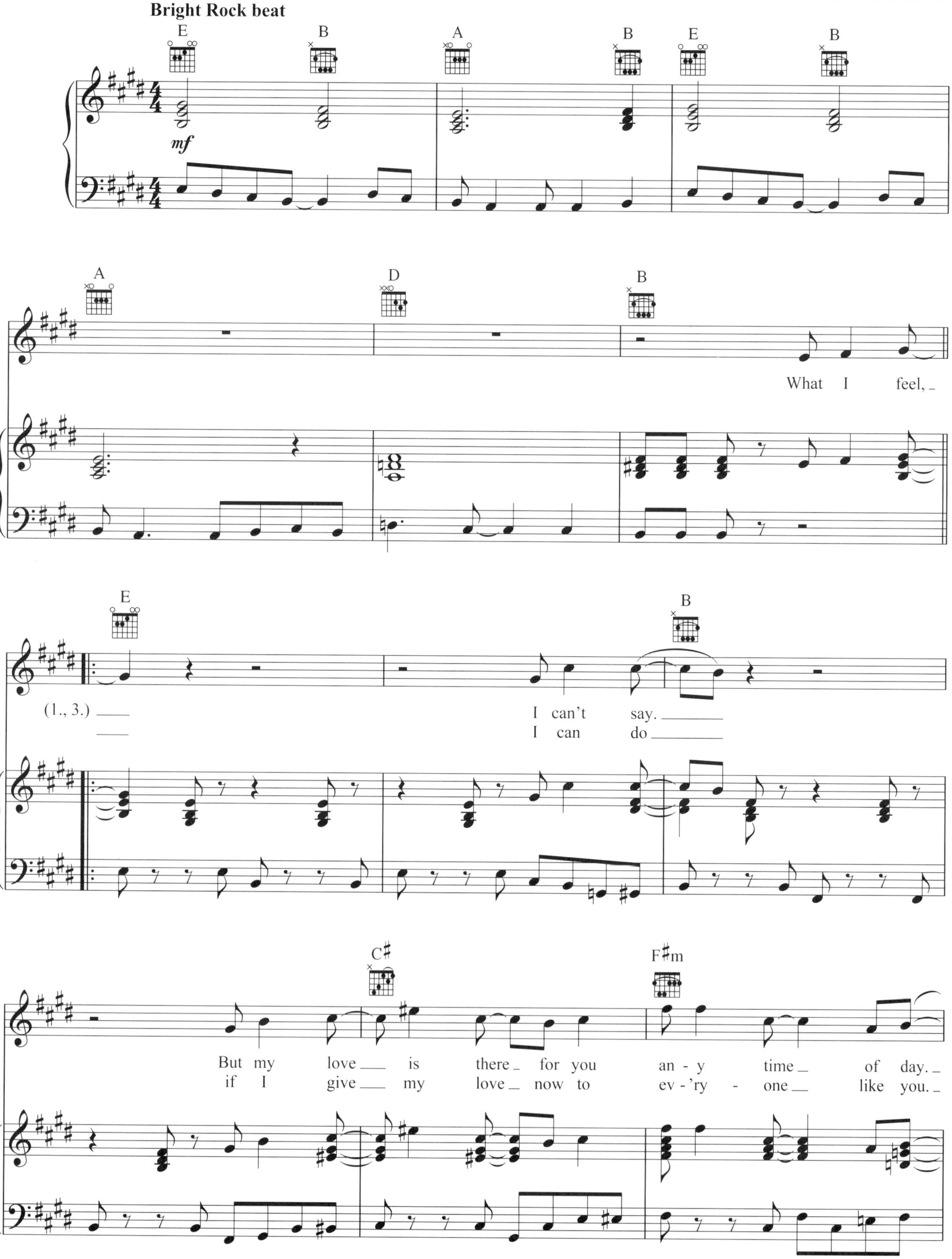

But if it's not love that you need, then I'll try my best to make ev-'ry-thing suc-ceed. And tell me, what is my life

A B E B A B
without your love?
And tell me,
E B A B
who am I without you
E B A D
by my side?
1, 3
B
What I know
2
D.S.
B
Tell me,
4
D.S. and Fade
B
Tell me,

YOU

Words and Music by
GEORGE HARRISON

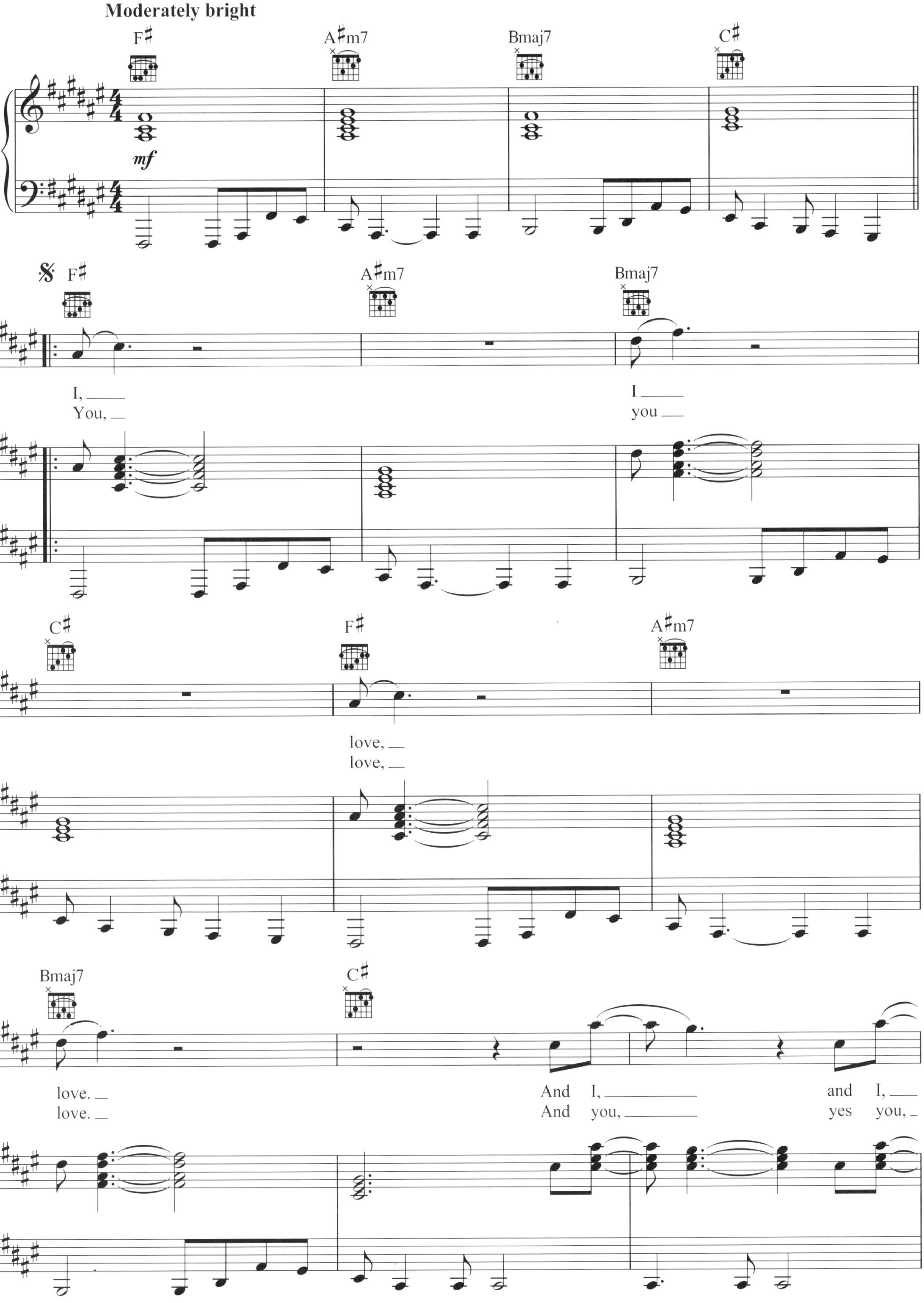

Lyrics:
I love you.
you love me.

Oh you, you,
Yeah you, you,

yeah you.
yeah you.

And when I'm hold-

B
A♯m
- in' you, ooh, what a feel - in'.
E
B
A♯m
Seems so good to be true that I'm tell - in' you all that I must
G♯m
C♯
F♯
A♯m7
be dream - in'.
Bmaj7
C♯
F♯
A♯m7

Lyrics: And I, and I, I love you, oh you, oh you, yeah you.

And when I'm hold - in' you, ooh,__ what a feel - in'.   Seems so good__ ___ to be true__ that I'm tell - in' you all__ that I must__ be dream - in'.

D.S. (verse 1) and Fade

WHO CAN SEE IT

Words and Music by
GEORGE HARRISON

Slowly

With pedal

I've been held up; I've been held down; I can see quite clear-ly now,
fear; I've been out there; I've been 'round and seen my share

through those past years,
of this sad world,

Copyright © 1973 The Material World Charitable Foundation Ltd. and Harrisongs Ltd.
Copyright Renewed
All Rights Reserved

when I ___ played "Toe - ing ___ the ___ Line." ___
and all ___ the hate ___ that ___ it's ___ stirred. ___

I on - ly ask that what I feel should not be
I on - ly ask that what I know should not be
ask that what I feel should not be

de - nied me now, as it's ___ been earned, ___
de - nied me now, as it's ___ been learned, ___
de - nied me now, as it's ___ been earned, ___

and I have seen: my life be - longs ___ to me; ___

my love be-longs ___ to who ___ can see ___ it.

I've lived in ___ can see ___ it.

279

WORLD OF STONE

Words and Music by
GEORGE HARRISON

Gospel Ballad

Wise man, you won't _ be to fol- -low the like _ of me in this

Copyright © 1975 Umlaut Corporation
Copyright Renewed
All Rights Reserved

281

| F | A |

world made ___ of stone, ___ such a long ___

| Dm | F/C | Asus | A7 |

___ way to go. ___

| Em | Bm |

We may dis-a-gree, we all ___

| Dm | F/C | B♭ |

___ have ___ the right ___ to be. In this

282

world made of stone, such a long way to go. Such a long, long way from home. Such a long

F
Asus
A7
way from home, such a
Dm7
F/C
Asus
A
long...
Em
Bm7
You may dis - a - gree, we all
Dm
F/C
B♭
have the right to be. In this

F
Bm7♭5
B♭dim7
A7
world made of stone. Such a long,
Dm
F/C
Asus
A7
long way to go. The
Em
Bm7
wis - er that you may be, the hard -
Dm
F/C
B♭
- er it can be to see. In this

world made of stone, such a long, long way to go. Such a long, way from home. In this world made of stone,

B♭dim7
A7
Dm
F/C
such a long, long, long way
Bm7♭5
F/A
G
F/A
B♭maj7
to go, such a long way from home.
Asus
A7
Em7
Bm7
Oh.
Dm7
F/C
B♭
F
(Such a long way from home.

Asus
A7
Dm7
F/C
Asus
A
Ah.)
Em7
Bm7
Dm7
F/C
B♭
F/C
Bm7♭5
B♭dim7
A7
Dm7
F/C
F
Repeat and Fade
Asus
A
Optional Ending
Asus
A